MarketPlace	: AUK	
Order Number	: 205-9824800-9313946	
Ship Method	: Standard	
Order Date	: 2013-12-09	
Email	: zyjkqrtw2qwsq7p@marketplace.amazon.co.uk	

Items : 1

Qty	Item	Locator
1	Sahara Man: Travelling with the Tuareg	MUL-2-EA-01-025-27
	ISBN : 0719561612	OD

RCode:

Please note:

Items are dispatched individually. If you have ordered multiple books they will

arrive in separate packages

We hope that you are completely satisfied with your purchase and ask you to leave positive feedback accordingly.

However, if you are unsatisfied with your order, please contact us by telephone or email. We will do whatever it takes to resolve the issue.

Mulberry House, Woods Way, Goring By Sea, West Sussex, BN12 4QY. Tel:+44(0)1903 507544
Email: sales@worldofbooks.com | Twitter: @WorldofBooksltd | Web: www.worldofbooks.com

be very sensitive to what it would almost certainly perceive as critic-
ism of its inability to guard its antiquities.

I had precisely eight days before my return flight to Tamanrasset.
Assuming I was able to organise supplies, donkeys and the obligatory
guide immediately, that would give me at best six days on the plateau.
To check out just the more significant sites, I would have to travel
about two hundred and fifty kilometres on foot over rugged terrain.
That meant about forty kilometres of walking each day, perhaps less if
I had a guide who knew the area really well.

Before we had reached his hotel Abdel Khader was throwing
himself enthusiastically into the details of my proposed trip and was
busily making plans. It was about four in the morning by the time we
arrived, but I wasn't allowed to tumble into my bed until we had sat
in his reception-cum-office for a while to clarify a few points. Keen
as he was to make all the arrangements (he was indeed desperate for
such business), he reckoned it was impossible to cover my proposed
route in so short a time. I assured him I was quite capable of walking
fast over long distances, as long as he could find me a young, fit guide
and enough donkeys to carry our provisions. By the time I had
snatched a couple of hours' sleep he had everything sorted out. The
guide, El Mouden, a young man in his late twenties, of very slight
and slender build, was at first not enthusiastic about my proposed
route. I had a feeling he was worried by my general physical state, and
he certainly made rather an issue of my age by continually referring
to me as *chaabani* (old man). Four donkeys and their driver, a young
man called Mohammed – I later learned he was only sixteen – were
also rounded up, leaving me with nothing more to do for the rest of
the day but look around Djanet and try to catch up on sleep. Abdel
Khader saw to it that food supplies, water and other equipment for
six days on the plateau were loaded into his Toyota and ready to leave
the hotel at five in the morning.

El Mouden and Mohammed were both members of the Kel
Medak and belonged to the Kel Ajjer Tuareg. Much less numerous
than the Kel Ahaggar, the Kel Ajjer today probably number no more
than a few thousand, many of them living across the border in Libya.
In the past I had spent very little time with the Kel Ajjer and conse-
quently knew them much less well than the Kel Ahaggar. Both

peoples speak the same language and share broadly the same culture, but in their history and in much of their outlook they are quite different. Historically the Kel Ajjer tended to look eastwards, towards Libya, rather than towards Ahaggar, and for long periods suffered warfare or raiding at the hands of the Kel Ahaggar.

Once the arrangements for my trek were in hand I was, briefly, tempted to catch up on sleep. But the prospect of seeing Djanet again was far too exciting, and I set off instead on a walk through the town. As I remembered it, Djanet was the most beautiful of all the desert oasis towns I had ever visited in the Sahara. It is still infinitely more picturesque than Tamanrasset, with its date groves and its more varied and highly-coloured stone and mud-brick houses, dotted in between the huge boulders strewn up the slopes of the rocky outcrops on which the little town is built along the side of the *oued*. Unlike Tamanrasset, it had not exploded in size since my last visit: the population had perhaps trebled. I set off down the main road that runs more or less from one end of the town to the other. Certainly there had been changes in thirty years. There was more traffic, more rush and bustle. And, as in Tamanrasset, I found myself preoccupied, almost subconsciously, with the satellite dishes protruding from nearly every rooftop. Walking along the bank of the *oued*, I was quite horrified by the tons of garbage that had been dumped into it to wait for the rains that would eventually come and flush the whole lot, disease and all, out into the sand seas of the great, limitless expanse of Sahara. Sometimes the rains didn't come for several years.

When I got back to the hotel about three hours later, a shock awaited me. Abdel Khader had told me that a few groups of tourists, mostly Germans and Italians, had begun to venture back into the region, but as I walked into the hotel's compound I was not expecting to bump into a whole contingent – about two dozen strong – of leather-clad Germans. About a dozen brightly painted motor-bikes were parked along one wall and a massive 'Germanic'-looking vehicle, resembling a cross between a militarised space crawler and a windowless double decker bus and sporting Bavarian number plates, blocked most of the entrance to the compound, while a dozen or so small but efficient-looking tents had sprung up over what was left of the space. There wasn't much room for anyone else. Abdel Khader was in the hotel's office, and I asked him where these apparitions had come from.

'It is a German company,' he explained, rather unnecessarily. 'The bikers cross the Sahara from Tunisia, keeping mostly to the Libyan side. They stow all their gear in the big truck, bike all day, and set up camp at night.'

'Have they just arrived?'

'Oh, no. They've been in the area for two or three days. They were down at Tadrart yesterday. The company's brought two groups through so far this winter.'

Wandering back to the compound I struck up a conversation with the Germans, and a group of us went into the hotel's restaurant for coffee. They were all very friendly, and having a wonderful time roaring around the Sahara on motor-bikes. One young couple had even brought their baby daughter with them. They had been up on the Tassili a couple of days before, to see some paintings. What had they thought of them, I asked? 'Pretty cool' was the husband's verdict, although he thought some of the colour was a bit faded. The young wife had been especially impressed by a painting of a negroid woman with breasts stippled all over in spots, as if tattooed. But what they had really liked was the way in which 'modern artists' had made their own contributions to the sites, which they saw as a sort of continuity of artistic expression from ancient man to the present day.

'What sort of "modern art" was it?' I asked, fearing the worst.

'Some new paintings,' he replied. 'Particularly of vehicles. And it's fun to try and read the names and dates.'

'Like graffiti?'

'Yeah. You could call them that.'

They were uncomplicated and friendly innocents-at-large. We talked a little longer about their plans for the rest of their journey further south, but my mind was already up on the plateau, trying to imagine what these 'modern artists' – an ironic euphemism for vandals if ever there was one – might have done to the sites.

To reach the plateau we had to climb about a thousand metres up the inward-facing scarp of the Tassili, which for most of its length is precipitous. We would take the Tafalelet Pass, the lowest of the four at just less than two thousand metres, the old camel route between Djanet and Ghat, used for countless ages by those crossing the plateau between these two oases for peaceful or warlike reasons. Bestriding the border between Algeria and Libya and marking the old interface between French and Turkish interests as it does, I doubt whether any other route in the Sahara has seen more 'history' pass along its tracks.

We drove to the base of the scarp in Abdel Khader's Land Cruiser. At six in the morning it was still dark, and cold enough for both sweater and anorak. The donkeys were already waiting for us; Mohammed had taken them there the previous evening and spent the night in an open camp. Loading them required time and skill, and I left it to El Mouden and Mohammed. The donkeys had a lot to carry: four large plastic jerricans of water, one big butane gas cylinder and its gas ring, two crates of food supplies and assorted utensils, blankets for the three of us, and our personal bits and pieces. But they were used to it, and only protested when the loads became unbalanced.

By the time we were ready the first light of dawn was breaking, and I could at last see my surroundings. They were monumental: the great cliff face of the Tassili scarp towered almost a thousand metres above us, and great sentinels of rock surrounded us on almost every side. As we moved off slowly up the pass, letting the donkeys set the pace, the first ray of sun lit the top of one of the great pillars of rock behind us, so that it stood out like a beacon. I stopped and turned to watch the sun's rays moving down its vertical face with the precision of a surgeon's knife, changing night into day and highlighting in microscopic detail the wafer-thin horizontal layers of ancient sandstone.

The climb up the pass was strenuous but not difficult, especially in the cold of the early morning. It was only dangerous if you missed your footing, but we didn't. This was the pass Henri Lhote had used to get his expedition's supplies and equipment up on to the plateau when he spent sixteen months there in 1956–7 recording the region's rock art. This sort of steep, rocky terrain is not really camel country, and his description of the torture and suffering through which he put his camels in climbing this pass makes very unpleasant reading. From his account of the expedition, it appears that at least eleven camels, possibly more, were killed in the course of these ascents, and that the Tuareg themselves eventually refused to provide him with any more.

After an hour and a half we came onto a flat and slightly sandy open area walled in by steep cliffs. Here and there we could look up into canyons, most of which were in dark shade as the sun only reached into them for a few short hours each day. Turning into one of them we followed it for a kilometre or so before turning into another and then another and another – all right-angled. After about an hour of this we made one last turn, almost completely back on ourselves, for the final and steepest ascent to the summit.

Climbing out of the gorge onto the plateau gave me a strange sensation of loss of balance. The sudden intense light may have had something to do with it, but I suspect it was more the effect of open space after nearly four hours in narrow canyons and gorges. The horizon was sky, and it was only a hundred metres away in each direction. The plateau seemed to fall away on all sides, leaving me with a feeling of being suspended above the earth. The entrance to Heaven might be a little like this. There were no reference points to get one's bearings by – no mountains, valleys, rock outcrops or sand seas – nothing except the flat black rock underfoot and the glaring sky above.

Mohammed and El Mouden unloaded the donkeys and let them wander freely. We were ready for a rest too, though I was pleasantly surprised by how well my body had stood up to the climb, and how fit I felt.

I first became aware of the Tassili in 1963 as an undergraduate at Cambridge University studying geography, and fortunate in having Claudio Vita-Finzi* as supervisor. Most of us undergraduates who knew Claudio, and I suspect even some of his academic seniors, regarded him as 'Renaissance Man' and listened enraptured to everything he had to say, especially about the Sahara, where he had just been on a combined Cambridge and Sheffield Universities expedition. Unfortunately they had not been able to visit the Tassili, which had recently come to world attention largely thanks to the publicity surrounding Henri Lhote's book *The Search for the Tassili Frescoes: The Rock Paintings of the Sahara.*

Claudio, interested in climatic change, prehistoric art and other related subjects, had written to Lhote expressing a desire to visit the Tassili and requesting a letter of introduction to the French military authorities in charge of the region. Lhote's reply was astounding, by

---

* Now Professor of Geology at University College, London.

any standards. It opened with a peremptory 'Dear Finzi' and proceeded to explain that since he, Henri Lhote, had discovered everything that there was to be discovered in the Tassili, there was no point in any other academic visiting the area. (This in itself was an interesting statement, because Swiss ethnologist Yolande Tschudi, to whom Lhote had made no reference at all, had explored the Tassili and published a book on the paintings there some time prior to Lhote's expedition.) Not only, therefore, would Lhote not provide the requested letter of introduction; he warned Claudio that if he insisted on visiting the region, he would use his influence with the military authorities to prohibit him access to the sites.

Lhote's letter was quite an eye-opener to an undergraduate just getting to grips with the ways of the academic world, but it did make me read his book. He may have drawn the world's attention to the Tassili, but he is not remembered with affection by the Tuareg on whom he was so dependent. He described them in the most racist, disparaging terms, referring to them as 'greedy', 'vain', 'begging', 'cunning', 'wretched', 'lacking in gratitude', comparing them with wolves and their laws with those of the 'forest or the jungle'.

I met Lhote once, in Tamanrasset in the 1960s. I was standing in the entrance to the old Hôtel Amenukal when the great man swept in, accompanied by his entourage. I extended my hand in greeting, and with the hope that he might have a moment in which to share some of his memories; he was, after all, perhaps France's greatest *Saharien*. But my hand was brushed aside like an irritating fly. Later, one of his entourage apologised, explaining that he was very deaf. I didn't ask about his eyesight.

I don't quite know what I expected to find on the Tassili this time. I was apprehensive that there might be a lot of damage – but also elated. Surely all who travel to this truly magical, almost mystical land high above the surrounding plains and sand seas feel similarly exhilarated, for there is probably nowhere else in the world where such a continuous, rich and all-embracing testimony to the life and artistic achievement of Neolithic man is to be found, set in a panorama that is itself breathtaking. Lhote's claim that the Tassili is the greatest museum of prehistoric art in the world is not easily challenged.

By mid afternoon, after a further two hours of easy walking across the plateau, we had reached the top of the *Oued* Tamrit, one of the many *oueds* that cut across the plateau, and stopped briefly at the first of the twenty or so ancient cypresses that still grow in the *oued*. This particular cypress, now officially listed as one of the twelve most threatened plant species in the world, is found only in this remote southern corner of the Tassili-n-Ajjer. An inventory undertaken in 1970–71 had registered 230 living and 153 dead specimens; I just wanted to touch this one, to make sure it was real.

The scientific name is *Cupressus sempervirens dupreziana*, named after the French military commander at Djanet, Captain Duprez, who came across the trees in the course of a military reconnaissance of the plateau in about 1920. One cannot say that he discovered the species, for it has always been known and used by the Tuareg, who call it *Tarout* and refer to it as the 'thirsty tree', as well as by the town dwellers of Ghat and Djanet, who have long used its wood for house doors and other objects. I ran my hand almost reverently over the thick, squat trunk of this great tree, only ten or so metres high, gnarled and beaten by the passage of time, knowing that it had almost certainly been here since before the time of the Prophet Mohammed. Absolute dating of the trees has not been possible, but along with the 'ancient pine' (*Pinus longaeva*) of the American north-west, the cypresses of the Tassili are considered to be among the oldest living trees in the world; the oldest has possibly survived as long as five millennia. Many of the trees I saw that day would have been growing at the time of Christ's birth, and would have witnessed the emergence of the ancient Saharan populations of Libya. The horse-drawn chariots of the Garamantes may even have been built from the wood of these trees. The Sahara can be a very humbling place.

Mohammed took the donkeys off on a short-cut to where we would be making camp for that night while El Mouden and I carried on, ambling rather than walking, down the *Oued* Tamrit. We had not gone far from the first cypress when we found ourselves in an amphitheatre-shaped basin where the *oued*'s sandy floor widened out into a 'stage' well over a hundred metres across. On our side of the *oued* its bank provided roughly tiered stone seating for spectators. The backdrop on the further side comprised resplendent, statuesque pillars thirty metres high sculpted by the elements – wind and water – from the ancient sandstone, whose colour changed with every new degree of the angle of the sun. Between the pillars, narrow defiles and the entrances to hidden canyons provided the wings of the 'stage' from which actors – or the ancient waters of millions of years – might spill out onto the stage. It was Petra, the Wadi Rum and other such places, all wrapped up in one.

That, at least, was how it might have been, how it should have been. But one side of the 'stage' was taken up with a mass of what looked like tumbledown scaffolding, and the natural rock shelters at the bases of the pillars – the entrances and exits – were almost all occupied by the brightly-coloured tents of a large party of Italian tourists whose equipment was scattered across the sand 'stage'.

'What is all that?' I asked El Mouden, pointing specifically at the scaffolding.

'Sonatrech,' he replied succinctly. Sonatrech is the Algerian state oil company, and for an outraged moment I thought it might actually be carrying out exploratory work in the area, following in Libya's footsteps in letting oil exploration loose even in antiquities-rich areas. El Mouden explained that Sonatrech either had used this breathtaking natural amphitheatre to stage some sort of *son et lumière* event for important guests, or was planning to do so. I was somewhat mollified. It sounded pretty corny, but no more depressingly vulgar than what many western corporates have perpetuated at one time or another in the name of 'art'. What I had taken for scaffolding were the metal frames of large tents, left in place.

I did not want to encounter the Italian tourists, nor was El Mouden keen that I should do so. I did not press him for his reasons, but presumed they involved some sort of code between guides about each sticking to his own patch. The adjoining areas of Libya, notably the Acacus Mountains, were beginning to be swamped by mass tourism from Italy, with devastating consequences for the rock art of the region, and for the environment generally. One camp site in the Acacus can hold six hundred at a time. (An archaeologist working in Libya later told me that fifteen thousand tourists had gone through Ghat between 20 December 1999 and 15 January 2000; I have not been able to confirm the figures, and prefer not to contemplate how their sewerage and rubbish were disposed of.)

As we made our way further on down the *oued*, from Upper to Lower Tamrit, the 'present day' was with us in abundance, mostly people's names (usually dated, which will at least make life easier for future archaeologists) scratched or painted willy-nilly all over the place – on the outside of shelters, in unpainted shelters and, worst of all, alongside or even on top of prehistoric paintings. Most seemed to belong to the 1980s, with few if any after 1992 – but there were already a few 1999s, presumably the fruits of the recent influx Abdel Khader had told me about. Perhaps technically these new additions were 'graffiti art', but to me they were nothing more than terrible vandalism, and unbelievably depressing; even writing about it moves me to tears. I began to take photographs – as if that would improve matters! – but after a while I gave up, except for some of the more grotesque examples. Most of the writing was in Italian, Arabic and French, with German running a poor fourth. English was pretty much a non-starter, since not many English-speakers (or English-writers) visit the region, but I felt pretty sure that if I scoured the plateau for long enough I would probably find an ode to Manchester United. One shelter, full of Neolithic paintings plus a splattering of the 'modern art' that had so impressed the young German travellers, had 'LOULOU' emblazoned in black paint along the bottom of the rock face. Loulou might have come from any one of a number of countries, but the name now encapsulates for me all that is mindless and idiotic about Western (and, for that matter, Arabic) culture.

The vandalism was not restricted to graffiti and daubings. Many of the paintings showed signs of having faded as a result of 'washing', and a few had been smudged or washed away beyond recognition. It was difficult for me to put a reliable measure on this. Not only was I relying on my memory and the prejudices of my first impressions, acquired more than thirty years previously, but I would need to have been able to compare photographs of exactly the same exposures, light intensities and so forth, which, with the exception of a couple of incidences at other sites, I was unable to do.

'Washing' a painting means literally that: throwing water over it or wiping it down with a wet cloth to remove the surface film of dust and dirt and temporarily enhance its colours. It is a tempting thing for tourists to do, especially as this was the technique used by Henri Lhote himself. He would wash the paintings to reveal the original colours, for his team of artists to copy onto paper tracings. These reproductions may now be seen at the Museum of Man in Paris and at the Bardo in Algiers in all their glory, but the practice is now totally outlawed. Such washing damages the paintings in at least three ways. The more a painting is washed, the more its original colour fades; washing removes the fine and almost invisible layer of lime-stone dust which, building up on the rock surface over time, acts like a varnish to protect the original paintings from the elements; and the wetting of the rock and its subsequent drying tends to draw the natural salts in the rock to the surface, thus accelerating its weather-ing. Lhote should be credited not so much with the 'discovery' of the Tassili paintings as with the onset of their degradation.

And as if such damage to the paintings were not enough, the *oued* itself was littered with the detritus of past tourists: old tin cans, bits of plastic, and empty wine, brandy and other spirit bottles, mostly French and Italian in origin.

I commented mildly on the damage to the paintings, and on the rubbish, but El Mouden showed little interest in either, and I let the subject drop. As far as he was concerned, his responsibilities extended to ensuring my safety and well-being (his continuing over-zealous concern for my age and physical state bordered on the irritating). His interest in the paintings was about on a level with Mokhtar's.

Later that afternoon one of the guides from the Italian group came down to chat with El Mouden and they sat in one of the shelters. As I joined them, El Mouden pointed to a couple of badly faded paint-ings on the brittle rock, giving them a sharp crack with his donkey stick, and asked his colleague and me what they represented. The other guide, completely uninterested, casually chucked a stone at the paintings. For a moment I saw red, and could quite easily have seized El Mouden's donkey stick and beaten them both about the head.

'Probably cattle,' I said, bitterly.

8

Tassili-n-Ajjer
the world's greatest collection of prehistoric rock art

THE NEXT MORNING, leaving Mohammed and the donkeys at our overnight camp, El Mouden and I set off on foot to a place called Tan Zoumiatek, about an hour away. Walking over much of the Tassili plateau is like walking over the high moors of Scotland with the heather stripped off. It is mostly flat, bare rock and the going is easy enough except in the occasional patches of sand deposited by the wind, sometimes piled into protected corners and hollows, to be moved around again next time it blows.

I hadn't slept well; my muscles had been over-tired from the previous day's exertions, my mind in a state of turmoil over what I had seen at Tamrit. El Mouden, too, was a little glum. I think he was aware of my disappointment of the previous day, however little he understood it. But the fresh morning air and the warmth of the early sun on my back raised my spirits, and whatever gloomy thoughts I still harboured were soon dispelled once we arrived at Tan Zoumiatek. Here, to my relief, there was no immediate sign of the damage or vandalism in the *Oued* Tamrit. On the contrary, I found myself walking almost hesitantly across the sand-covered floor of an open-air art gallery whose sculpted rock walls, here rising like castellated turrets, there almost closing over high above us, displayed paintings of almost indescribable beauty and depths of symbolism. The poise and balance of two dancing women were so finely captured by the creator(s) of one fresco that I could almost hear the singing and clapping and feel the rhythm of the dance. Two elegantly slender, exquisitely coiffed and bejewelled women nearby could have graced any contemporary catwalk. The greatest beauty of these women was perhaps their negritude. These people, referred to by Lhote as 'Martians' and by subsequent archaeologists and ethnologists as 'Round Heads' because of their predominantly round and often oversized heads, were unmistakably Negroid. They were the inaugurators of the Neolithic revolution in this part of the Sahara at the end of the last Ice Age, some twelve or thirteen thousand years ago. They invented pottery, the remains of which can still be found scattered over the ground, they attempted to domesticate wild animals and, from what we can tell from the complex symbolism of much of their art, it would seem that they had highly developed ritual and religious belief systems.

Just around the corner – in the next gallery, entered by passing between a series of statuesque rock pillars and wind-eroded arches – was a magnificent *mouflon* painted in dark red etched in white, strong and with massive, perfectly curved horns. Just above it was a symbol variously described by ethnologists as a 'medusa' or a 'jellyfish'. It clearly represents something that was of fundamental importance to these prehistoric peoples because it is found, almost like a stamp, alongside or superimposed on countless paintings throughout the region. Sometimes it does indeed look like a jellyfish; elsewhere it is more of a spiral, or a circle with one or more circles inside it. Sometimes it appears to have horns, and a little imagination can perhaps discern an eye at its centre. More frequently, it merely looks like the ectoplasm of popular spiritualist imagery. What it symbolises is uncertain, the subject of widespread debate among ethnologists. Some have interpreted it as the sun, or as a cloud, with the tentacles hanging down beneath it representing rain. Others, probably correctly, see it as some sort of symbolisation of creation and the life form.

The state of the paintings at Tan Zoumiatek was so fine that I dared to hope the damage in the *Oued* Tamrit might perhaps be localised; Tamrit, after all, was the nearest site to Djanet, and the most accessible to tourists. Tan Zoumiatek was just a little further away and slightly more inaccessible and so, I reasoned (or hoped), the damage from tourists probably diminished the further one went across the plateau.

But I was sadly mistaken. As we trekked on through that day and the next, through places of which I had no previous record but which El Mouden dutifully named for me – Ouan Ghofar Tamarit, Initinen, Ouan Etuharni – the gloom returned. Most of the rock art sites we passed were terribly depressing. Admittedly they were not the most celebrated sites in the Tassili, but many of the paintings had clearly been so 'washed' that they had faded beyond recognition, and there was 'modern art', nearly all in red or black, with Tuareg (*tifi-nagh*), Arab and European graffiti daubed all over.

At Tin Tazarift, however, the well-known fresco of the Round Head archers was still a sight of absolute perfection. These archers, who appear to be floating across a rock face, have been dated as belonging stylistically to the middle of the 'Round Head' period, around ten thousand years ago. They appeared quite untouched by modern man, apart perhaps from a 'washing'. It almost seemed that the vandalism was in some way 'selective', restricted to sites of lesser magnificence, lesser artistic importance. Perhaps the vandals were not wholly lacking in appreciation or sensitivity. If this was so, I might expect to find little vandalism at the 'high points' of Tassilian rock art, places such as Sefar, Jabbaren and Ouarenhat, places all still before me.

We reached Sefar on the evening of our third day, approaching it along the narrow *oued* that runs into it. As we did so, no more than thirty metres ahead of us a *mouflon* jumped out from some rocks. It was the first *mouflon* I had ever seen, and a splendid sight, half sheep, half mountain goat, with a bit of antelope thrown in for good measure. Its horns were almost the size of its body, thick and heavy at the base and curling back in perfect symmetry in a complete semicir-cle so that their tips all but touched its back. It stood for a second or two, obviously surprised, before darting off between the rocks and out of sight. A few minutes later, as we sounded a corner in the *oued* to emerge through a rocky defile into a slightly more open area, a herd of seven *mouflon* ran in front of us. They were gone before I had even thought of my camera. The mere sight sent El Mouden into ecstasy. There is something about the *mouflon*, much more than just the thrill of the hunt and the taste of the meat, that lifts Tuareg onto an almost spiritual plane.

We camped that night in rock shelters eroded out of the base of the low cliffs that bounded the *oued* some four hundred metres before it turned into Sefar. Underneath the daubs of tourists who had evidently stayed in these same shelters I could make out earlier, prehistoric paintings. Another saddening sight. While El Mouden and Mohammed prepared our evening meal, I wandered up the *oued* in the opposite direction to Sefar. There too, one had not far to seek for the debris left by tourists of earlier years, piles of old tin cans and bottles stashed away in the nooks and crannies between boulders. As had become my habit, I began to photograph them. The thought in the back of my mind was that by collecting pictorial evidence of what tourism had done to this precious environment, I could perhaps go on to do something about it. I wondered how future archaeologists would judge us. They must surely see the tin can and glass bottle as central to our civilisation. It was a dreary thought.

My immediate study involved noting whatever marks of origin remained on the rubbish. Most was French and Italian in origin, but the prize for originality went to a large tin of preserved ham made for Komsomol by the Czechoslovak Ministry of Foodstuff. 'Ministry of Foodstuff' was written thus in English and the use of the singular was presumably a translation error, for even under Communism there had been a modicum of variety in the tinned goods produced in Czechoslovakia. Was it Czechs who had left it there, or was it one of their export products brought to the Tassili by others? Whoever was responsible, ham was not the most diplomatic comestible to bring to a Moslem country.

Like most of the litter I had already seen scattered over the Tassili, the rubbish at the approach to Sefar seemed to have been there for several years. On the silver lining principle, at least Algeria's crisis had, temporarily anyway, stopped tourists from further despoiling the region.

We all went to bed early. It was very cold, and I wanted to be up early to enter Sefar. I had not been long asleep when I was awakened by horrific, high-pitched screams. All I could think of was babies having their throats slit – not, thank goodness, that I have ever heard such a sound. The knowledge that I was in a country where so many people have been killed in this way must have overstimulated my imagination. But such screams are disconcerting anywhere, and I listened to them for several seconds, my heart racing, before I realised that they were made by a pack of jackals. The screaming of jackals in the middle of the night is a most eerie and scary sound, and one I had not heard for more than thirty years. They were not far away, and I wondered if they had been attracted by our presence. I opened my tent flap, feeling the sting of freezing air on my face, and looked towards the shelter where El Mouden and Mohammed were sleeping. They had not roused themselves, so I returned to the warmth of my sleeping bag. At four the screams began again, but this time I at least knew what they were, and merely listened to the hideous din as they fought among themselves.

Sleep was gone for good, however, so I got up early, keen to take some photographs in the first light of dawn. Dressing warmly, I picked up my camera and clambered out of my tiny tent. El Mouden and Mohammed were still fast asleep under their blankets. The air was freezing, but beautifully clear in the early dawn. The sun's rim was just about to emerge above the horizon. I climbed up the low cliff onto the rocks above the shelter, the rubber soles of my boots making no noise.

Yes! Right there, not more than a hundred metres in front of me, perched statuesquely on a rock, was a *mouflon*, presumably one of the herd we had seen the previous evening. There was no wind, and therefore little chance that it would pick up my scent. I moved my hand agonisingly slowly to flick open my camera case, determined to make no move or sound that would frighten it. I eased the camera up to my face, keeping my gaze fixed on the beast. It did not move. Would it hear the camera shutter and run? No: it remained perched on its rock, looking straight ahead. I wanted to pee, but that would have to wait. I moved indescribably slowly, inching my way over the rugged terrain, placing one foot delicately in front of the other, careful not to disturb any loose stone or make any sudden move. I checked my camera, carefully and slowly: there was an entire film in it. These were the sort of photographs that never came out of the Sahara. Forward, slowly: eighty metres ... seventy ... sixty. Still the camera shutter did not alarm it. Fifty metres, forty metres. It was a big animal, maybe big enough not to be afraid. Still it did not move. Thirty metres, twenty metres. I had almost finished the film. The *mouflon* must be very old, perhaps deaf and maybe even a little blind. No one, I was sure, had ever been so close to one in the wild.

I am not quite sure how or when I realised that my *mouflon* was a sculpted outcrop of rock: I had left my spectacles in my tent. I thanked God that neither El Mouden nor Mohammed had seen me.

Not far from my *mouflon* I found the source of the jackals' interest. They had come across a dead donkey, not one of ours, and ripped it to pieces. All that remained were the head and a stump of spinal column, the blood still crimson.

Sefar is, for me at least, the most awesome of all the Tassili's secrets, surpassing even Jabbaren in its grandeur. In simple geological terms, Sefar is a sandstone massif perhaps a couple of kilometres in length and about half as wide, so cut through by water erosion that it is now a maze of narrow gorges and defiles hollowed out from the blocks of sandstone and cascading, sometimes precipitously, from one level to another. Some form narrow alleys, some streets, while yet others open out into grand boulevards lined with giant stone pillars and leading into great piazzas and amphitheatres. Lhote had likened the surrounding rock formations to the temples of Angkor Wat, and Rheims Cathedral after it was bombarded in the First World War. In among the tangled forest of rock pillars are a number of permanent rock waterholes, or *gueltas*, and many more which are seasonal. The whole is like a city: more dramatic, more hidden, and more beguiling than Petra.

Sefar is magic. One need only read Lhote's map of it to know that, for all his failures, he felt it too: L'Arc de Triomphe, Le Grand Sanctuaire, La Grotte Bleue, Place Bacchus, La Femme accroupie, L'Avenue de la Dune, Rue de Petits Mouflons, Place du Panorama, Cirque du Lion, Le Grand Dieu, Place de la Mosquée, Esplanade du Dieu Pécheur, Rue de la Négresse, Rue des Cannes á Boules, and more. He scarcely exaggerated. One walks through these places, intoxicated by their splendour, down streets and into side alleys lined not by shops, restaurants and bars but by the caves and rock shelters in which the ancient Neolithic inhabitants of this extraordinary place once dwelt – certainly in their hundreds, perhaps even in thousands – and applied their art. I left El Mouden, deliberately allowing myself to become swept up and lost in the almost other-worldly atmosphere. For just a day I would be the only inhabitant – except for the ghosts, and the wild animals.

The best-known fresco at Sefar, perhaps in the entire Tassili complex, is the one Lhote called 'Le Grand Dieu'. This elaborate work covers the wall of a rock shelter some sixteen metres in width and about four or five metres high, and is dominated by 'Le Grand Dieu' himself, standing about three and a quarter metres high and surrounded by and overlain with a range of other paintings both beautiful to the eye and rich and complex in their symbolic meaning. It had been washed, of course, by Lhote's team and perhaps by visitors after him, but otherwise it showed no signs of vandalism or damage and was exactly as I remembered it ... except that there *was* something different about it. For a moment, I could not figure out what was wrong. Then I saw them: two dark rectangles, painted in what looked like some sort of oil or varnish, one about seventy-five centimetres wide and forty-five high on the God's stomach and to its side, the other covering the chest of the reddish-hued antelope to his right. At Tamrit there were frescos damaged in just this way, but they were relatively insignificant paintings of humans or cattle, and I had assumed that someone had been trying to make a transfer of them, or heighten the colour. I stared at 'Le Grand Dieu', trying to absorb all its magnificence and complexity – the horns, the ectoplasm, the loincloth, the ambivalent sexuality, the suppliant woman, the obvious fertility symbols, and the animals superimposed over and alongside it – and wondered who could have spoilt such a great work of art in this way.

And then I remembered: a team of scientists working with UNESCO had attempted to protect the paintings from further erosion by applying a varnish-like resin substance to them. It had been done, if memory served, in the late 1960s, and that was what I was now looking at. Sealing the rock, as any 'scientist' should know, would merely serve to trap moisture beneath the surface and hasten its deterioration. But why ever did they choose to experiment at the very centre of the greatest painting in the entire Tassili? Was it the arrogance of supposed 'experts', or sheer stupidity? I remembered the words of an artist friend who lives at Fountainebleau. I had asked her husband, a Professor of Political Economy at INSEAD, Europe's prestigious business school, how the twentieth century would be remembered; she had immediately replied, 'For its vandalism.'

I was running out of time. I had had a mere six days in which to search the Tassili, and only two remained. We trekked southwards across the plateau through the Tisouar hills, where the sand dunes were piled up against their jagged black castellated crests, past Tin Keni, Ala-n-Edoument and on towards Jabbaren Jabbaren, at about two thousand metres, the highest point in this part of the Tassili, is where one finds the greatest abundance of rock paintings. To our left, no more than sixty kilometres away, was Libya. Below the crest of the

Tassili and out of sight was the oasis of Ghat. Beyond it and filling the eastern horizon were the Acacus mountains, standing out soft and pink in the afternoon sun, a marked contrast to the burnt, black surface of the Tassili. I was sorely tempted to change direction. I could make Ghat in a day; another would get me to the Acacus, where I knew from the Internet that paintings had recently been hacked out of the rock. But I had no visa, and doubted that the Libyan authorities would take too kindly to a casual dropper-in. And the Algerians might not allow me back. The temptation proved after all no more than a passing whim. I was here for the very specific purpose of seeing whether the Tassili paintings had suffered the same fate as those across the border. The trail of litter and what might be described as 'low-level' vandalism was immensely distressing, but at least I had not yet come across any sites where paintings had actually been hacked out of the rock face. Nor had any of the best-known frescos been seriously vandalised.

I had just two days to reach Jabbaren and search the area. My feelings were somewhat mixed. To find tangible evidence of such damage would satisfy my 'detective' instincts and, more importantly, could be used to draw attention to these crimes. On the other hand, it was horrendous to think of any of the paintings there being hacked out of the rock and sold into a private collection somewhere.

Jabbaren, once a prehistoric Neolithic community in the mould of Sefar, is perched on the northern side of a deep valley, the *Oued* Amezzar, which cuts across this section of the plateau, draining its waters – when occasional storms bring them – eastwards into Libya. We arrived in the evening and made camp in a series of rock shelters cut into the cliffs along the side of the *oued* a few hundred metres away from the main complex. The shelter El Mouden chose was a ghastly sight, dominated by a huge black swastika-like emblem perhaps a metre across, painted on the rock wall. Around it and covering most of the rest of the shelter was a mass of the most hideous daubs and scribblings I had yet seen. The script was mostly European and Arabic, with a smattering of modern-day *tifinagh*. Beneath all this mess, one could just make out the vestiges of some prehistoric paintings. I half expected a troop of Hitler Youth to appear and order us to move on, but in any case had already decided to set my tent up elsewhere, for the shelter was open to the wind, and it was beginning to pick up. I moved to another, smaller and unpainted, about fifty metres around the corner.

The wind did not persist, and by morning a lot of cloud had gathered over the plateau. I wondered if we would get rain. My plan was to search the sites around Ouarenhat on the far side of the *oued* in the early morning, returning to search Jabbaren in the afternoon. We set out early, grateful for the cloud cover as we clambered perhaps a hundred metres down the steep, boulder-strewn side of the Amezzar valley and then up its even more arduous southern side. I was faintly surprised not to see vehicle tracks on the *oued*'s sandy floor, as the valley appeared to provide direct access to Libya. If anyone wanted to make a quick sortie into the Jabbaren area through the back door, this was the way to come.

It may have been my imagination, or perhaps my memory was playing tricks, but it seemed that many of the more important paintings at Ouarenhat had faded badly, presumably from being repeatedly washed. To my delight, however, my favourite painting was still there, and undamaged. It was small, only about twenty-five centimetres across but exquisitely painted, of a couple making love in the kneeling position. Even El Mouden commented favourably on it, giving it a crack of approval with his donkey stick. It is somehow reassuring to know that the sources of human pleasure have changed little over the millennia.

Climbing back up to Jabbaren's craggy rock ramparts with their strange beehive-shaped tops was heavy going. Certainly I was tired after walking about thirty kilometres a day for several days, I think it was more the result of a tremendous sense of anticlimax. The Tassili is unique – one might almost count it as one of the wonders of the world – but in a few short years it has been reduced to what my artist friend at Fontainebleau would describe as the hallmark of the twentieth century. What has been done here is truly shameful.

My mind was again in turmoil. It was such a paradox. How could I not feel pleased that I had failed to find the terrible evidence I needed to make my case? I had only Jabbaren left to search, and the likelihood of finding the evidence I sought at this 'high point' of Tassilian rock art was small.

*

It would be unfair to ask anyone who knows the Tassili to choose a favourite painting: the variety of styles and content, epoch and symbolism is too immense. If I had to plump for one, it would be the painting of the story of Tyanaba at Jabbaren. The story of Tyanaba is a myth of the Fulani people who now live along the southern fringes of the Sahara, more than sixteen hundred kilometres to the southwest of the Tassili, and was first recorded by the French anthropologist Germaine Dieterlen in 1966, recounted to her by elders of the Fulani tribe; the painting at Jabbaren depicts the story of Tyanaba in the same immaculate detail.

Tyanaba is the goddess responsible for the health and well-being of the Fulani's cattle herds. In the myth, and as the painting reveals, Tyanaba takes the form of a serpent and emerges from lakes and rivers to wrap herself around the best milch cow or leading bull in a herd. The heads of seven sheep emerge from the front of her body, each representing the seven sons of Kikala and Nagara, the first human couple created by Guéno. The painting also shows five exquisitely depicted girls, the mythical sisters of the seven sons, to the right of Tyanaba, grouped within a sinuous thread. The final component of the picture is another creation of Guéno, a hermaphroditic 'bull' with a head at either end, which appears to be almost enveloped by Tyanaba. The Fulani say it is the mythical ancestor of all cattle.

Parts of the painting, notably the seven sheep's heads and one head of the bicephalic beast, have almost disappeared, though they can be clearly seen on Lhote's original tracings. The remarkable similarity between the way the five girls and present-day Fulani women wear their hair and the fact that the painting at Jabbaren depicts the Fulani myth of Tyanaba in every detail are strong evidence of the ancestral link between the prehistoric pastoralists of the Tassili and the pastoral Fulani peoples of the Sahel.

I sat on the floor of the shelter for a long time, looking at the detail of the painting and thinking how extraordinary it was that something so many thousands of years old should still be so alive today in the myths of people living so far away.

There was not much else for me to see. I had explored most of Jabbaren; the wind was getting up again and I could see that El Mouden was anxious to get back to our camp. I decided to walk the 'main street', the *oued* that runs through Jabbaren, one last time, to pay my respects to what Lhote christened the 'Great Martian God'. The painting occupies the entire wall of the 'great shelter' on the left bank of the *oued*, and is a little difficult to see unless one stands well back from it, because of the simplicity of its outline and its enormity – it is about six metres in height.

I gazed my fill, and as I turned to walk away something caught my attention on the other side of the 'street'. Not sure what it was, I strolled over, peering about. Why had I failed to notice anything amiss when I walked down the street earlier? Perhaps it was a trick of the light – but no! There it was – or, rather, wasn't. Someone had hacked a painting out of a shelter in the 'main street' of Jabbaren, perhaps the most revered site in the whole context of Saharan pre-history.

The deed had not been done with anything as sophisticated as a chain-saw. It looked as though a simple cold chisel with a half-inch blade had been used, and the chisel marks looked pretty fresh. Only half the painting, which was of a herd of cattle, had been removed. It was on the roof of the cave, almost where a cornice might have been, at the intersection of three natural fissures. These, and the weathered rock at the side of the painting, had provided the lines of weakness into which the chisel blade had been inserted.

I felt numb with shock, but my own personal paradox was resolved: I was not pleased that my intuition had proved correct and given me my evidence. On the contrary, when the shock had eased, blazing anger and great sadness took over, and I wanted to get off the plateau as soon as possible. I inspected the gash in minute detail and photographed it from every conceivable angle, like a forensic pathologist working over a corpse. All the while I was wondering who had done this terrible thing, and what they were thinking while they did it. Had they any idea of the enormity of their crime? I say 'they', because the missing rock must have weighed about fifty kilos and would not have been easy for one person to carry away on his own.

That evening we sat around the campfire preparing our meal of vegetable stew mixed with *tagella*. The wind was beginning to gust quite strongly, and as the fire flared it threw weird dancing shadows over the wall of the rock shelter. The black swastika seemed to wave at us fanatically. For our own very different reasons, we all wanted to get off the plateau as soon as possible. El Mouden had been married for only a few months, and this was the first paid work he had had in that time. Excited at the prospect of getting back to Djanet, he told me all about the bright new materials he was going to buy his wife.

I just wanted to get back to Tamanrasset. I had seen the splendours of the Tassili's paintings for myself once again; they were still magnificent, but tarnished now. The darker side of the jumbled motives that had taken me to Tassili had, to my sorrow, found its justification. Now I had to think what to do about it, and that was not easy. I felt muddled-headed. It might have been the bitter, piercing cold brought on the wind, or the residue of shock. As we sat eating our last meal together in the wan light of the dying fire, I contemplated the extraordinary part pure chance had played in my discovery of the stolen painting. For six days I had searched, I had trekked close on two hundred and forty kilometres, and it was not until the last hour of the last afternoon that I had found my evidence. I could so easily have missed it. What *was* it that had caught my attention and made me cross the 'main street' again? I like to think I am not superstitious, but the more I thought about it, the more convinced I became that Something had drawn me across that short distance.

We agreed that we would break camp at first light and start our descent as soon as the donkeys were loaded. They too would probably be glad to get off the plateau, for it was spartan country with very little pasture for them. Not long after eight I made my way to my own shelter, where my little tent looked as though it might take off in the wind at any minute. I checked the tent pegs and put a few boulders over them to be on the safe side. Because of the wind it seemed no warmer inside the tent, and I slid into my sleeping bag in all my clothes. I was soon wakened from an uneasy sleep by the billowing and flapping of the tent in the wind, and a strange knocking noise like large stones being banged together. Probably it was the rocks over the tent pegs. I knew I would not sleep if they were not dealt with, so I eased myself out of my sleeping bag and braved the bitter night air. None of the rocks I had put in place seemed to be moving, but I rearranged them nevertheless and scurried back into my sleeping bag. The temperature was already below zero.

Needless to say, the more I craved sleep, the more sleep fled, and I slipped into one of those wretched, nightmarish trains of thought that bedevil such hours. The starting point was the stolen painting, and that took me to Algeria's crisis, following the thread of logic which suggested that if there had been no troubles in the north the Tassili would not have been emptied of tourists and guides, so the opportunities for hacking out paintings would not have presented themselves so readily.

Thoughts of the war in the north brought back the image of the man on the flight to Djanet whose throat had been slit. From there it was no distance to the rebels fighting the government: if their goal was to bring down the government, or at the least to cause it maximum disruption and difficulty, especially on the international stage – why not kill a few foreigners? Why not, indeed. According to most reports on the country, that was exactly what they had been trying to do, but Algeria's tight security and a dearth of foreigners entering the country meant that few had actually been killed. I began to replay in my mind all the advice I had been given in London about how risky this trip would be, how potentially dangerous it was. The British Embassy in Algiers had hit the top notes in a crescendo of disapproval when I telephoned to seek advice on travelling in the south. And those up-to-the-minute security reports I had read on the Internet just before my departure – they had referred to new 'incidences' in the south-east of the country. *This* was the south-east of the country!

Travelling with Mokhtar, such fears had not entered my head. Travelling in the company of Tuareg is one of the safest feelings in the world. But now, here on the Tassili, all sense of security suddenly began to drain away. I found myself thinking what I would do if *I* were such a terrorist: I would travel through Libya and re-cross the border into Algeria right here in the south-east, where there are no border controls: I would lie in wait in the *Oued* Amezzar for tourists foolish enough to ignore the advice of their governments to stay away from Algeria; as they camped out at night around Jabbaren, the 'high point' of prehistoric artistic achievement (a nice symbolic touch), I would slit their throats and leave their corpses to be found – if the jackals didn't get them first – by the Algerian *gendarmerie* who would assuredly come in search of them when they failed to return to Djanet.

This was nightmare stuff, but I was wide awake, and beginning to feel the chill of real fear. My tent was a dangerous place. The wind was growing stronger; the stones were still knocking, and I suddenly noticed eerie flashes of light over the roof and walls of my tent. I would be safer outside. Once more I crawled out into the freezing night air, clutching my torch as my only weapon. There was no one there. What a fool my over-strung thoughts were making of me! And that flashing light was nothing more sinister than the moon, shining through breaks in the scudding clouds. It was only ten o'clock, and there were more than eight hours of darkness to go. I wandered about, then around the corner to El Mouden's shelter. He and Mohammed were asleep on the ground beneath the swastika, covered by thick blankets, seemingly oblivious to the commotion of the night. No one had slit their throats. Crossing the flat, sandy floor of the *oued* I sat in a rock shelter under one of the cliffs on the other side. I needed to calm my nerves. I would sit here for a while and let the night become familiar – the light of the moon coming and going from behind the clouds, the wind, the freezing cold, and that strange knocking of the stones, which so far I had only heard when I was in my tent.

After a while I returned to my tent, now merely irritated by my own stupidity. Once more I tried to sleep. My thoughts drifted back to the stolen painting, but this time to the people who had painted it, and to those who had inhabited this weird and extraordinary place. Like Sefar, it had been a Neolithic 'city'. Over the course of twelve or thirteen millennia, this place must have been home to many thousands of people – men, women and children. What would they think if they could see how their legacy had been despoiled? Surely their spirits must linger here? If I were such a spirit, I know that I would be angry. But not with someone like me, because I was on their side. The spirits would protect me because I understood their anger and what had caused it, and because I might even perhaps be able to do something about it, to appease them. Thinking about the spirits of the people of Jabbaren made me feel calmer, but still I could not sleep. The wind and the rocks were too noisy, and my brain refused to shut down.

Then I remembered: in the bottom of my rucksack was a book, forgotten about until this moment. Claudia had a small collection of English novels in her house in Tamanrasset, and I had borrowed it 'in case'. Now was the time! With the aid of my penlight I dug it out – David Lodge's *Changing Places*. It was amusing, but critical literary

140

appraisal didn't come into it: I was reading for purely practical purposes, to take my mind off terrorists, spirits, and the distractions and discomfort of my immediate surroundings.

It was about midnight and I was well into my book when I became aware of a chilliness about the backside. I shifted a little, the inch or so a sleeping bag allows, but it crept slowly down the backs of my thighs to my knees and up towards the lower reaches of my back. The knocking, of which I had been unaware while reading, persisted though the wind, I noticed, had dropped: evidently I was not suffering from wind-chill. I put up with this new trial for some time before sitting up to investigate. My wonderful 'Rolls-Royce' sleeping bag with its triple-zip system had split! It had never been completely unzipped, because I had taken to getting in and out of it by sliding in and out of the opening at the top, in order to preserve the warmth, yet all three zips had come apart in the middle, opening up a bottom-sized gap. I couldn't see what was wrong in the limited light, and try as I might, I couldn't get any of the zips to close – in fact, the opening lengthened, leaving me with more of a single eiderdown than a sleeping bag. I put on a second pair of trousers and my storm anorak, and wrapped the 'eiderdown' around me. Thus protected from the cold, and with David Lodge's assistance, I saw out the rest of the night.

Some people believe that a sudden drop in temperature indicates the arrival of a ghost. For all my talk of 'spirits', however, I do not believe in ghosts ... and yet ... When I got home, I returned the sleeping bag to its suppliers. They refunded my money, but I'm fairly sure they did not believe that I had never undone the zips. Examining it, they found wrench marks, described as being 'like teeth marks', at intervals of roughly one foot along the entire length of each zip.

I am still disinclined to believe in ghosts, but if they do exist, then Jabbaren is the place to encounter them.

We awoke in the morning to find that the wind had ceased, and thick cloud had closed in around us. A storm was coming, and to stay on the plateau any longer than necessary was to court certain discomfort and possible disaster. As fast as the donkeys could manage we crossed the few remaining kilometres of the plateau between Jabbaren and the top of the gorge at the Col d'Aroum, down which we were to make our descent. A soft drizzle began to fall, and visibility was no more than a few hundred metres. I was not tempted to savour the conditions, rare as such weather is in the Sahara, because I had experience of the force of the sort of storm they probably presaged, and did not relish being caught in one again. It was bitterly cold. If the heavens were to open at this moment the descent would be dangerous, for the gorge we had to negotiate could turn within minutes into a raging torrent.

The gorge plunged steeply through a thousand metres, straight down and boxed in to almost touching distance by the sheer vertical walls of the Tassili's huge escarpment. Behind and above us the great mass of black, sodden cloud clung to the plateau, as if undecided what to do with itself but reluctant to venture too far out from the plateau into the empty sky beyond. In front of us there was clear sky and sun, slanting down onto the sea of sand dunes that begins about fifteen kilometres out into the desert beyond Djanet. The dunes cast their own shadows, making it difficult to tell the difference between the dunes and the valleys between them and giving a dappled effect to the desert surface. Eight hundred kilometres away and almost directly in front of us was Tamanrasset.

We made the descent in under three hours, which was fast going, and would have been quicker but for the donkeys, which tended to set the pace. Our rendezvous with Abdel Khader was set for midday, which gave us just enough time to unload the donkeys and sort out all the baggage. El Mouden found a couple of oranges we'd over-looked, and I ensconced myself on a large flat-topped boulder to eat one while I contemplated the scarp. A short distance to the left of the gorge we had just negotiated was a place where a huge section of rock had broken away and come crashing down. It looked quite recent to me, but when I asked El Mouden if he knew when it had happened, he said it had always been like that.

Abdel Khader – ever businesslike – arrived bang on time, and I was back at the Hôtel Zeriba half an hour later. I didn't tell him about the stolen painting, uncertain how he would take it: his whole business and future depended on tourism. He deserved to succeed – he had ensured that there was hot water in the hotel shower. In the Sahara, luxury is a shower: warm water, soap and shampoo are added bonuses. For twenty minutes I revelled in all three, then got rid of a week's stubble.

The hotel's cook rustled me up an omelette and some fresh bread, which I took out to one of the plastic-topped tables on what could, with a little imagination, be described as the patio. I moved the table to a corner sheltered by a fading bougainvillaea which seemed to entertain hopes of escaping frost for another year. From there I could look up to the foothills below the Tassili's scarp. The cloud and drizzle we had trekked through that morning looked even more ominous. At any minute the heavens would open and the waters would come cascading off the plateau and down through the gorges. But I was clean, warm and relaxed; my only immediate concern was how to spend the afternoon and evening, for the flight to Tamanrasset did not leave until one in the morning.

There would not be much sleep for me during the coming night, but I decided to go for a long walk through the town again, this time in the knowledge that the rains were on their way, and that within a matter of hours the tons of garbage in the *oued* would be flushed out and dumped in the desert beyond.

It was mid-afternoon by the time I had walked back into town, chatting on the way to a man, perhaps in his forties, who told me he was an engineer, just down from Algiers to look into ways of establishing Internet facilities here in Djanet and in Tamanrasset. Telephones, satellite television, soon the Internet: change, when it comes, can come very fast.

Just as I was about to turn in to the hotel I noticed a middle-aged European couple sitting at one of the tables of the street café, more or less in the middle of the town and clearly something of a communal meeting-place. Our eyes met, and they waved. I didn't really want to get engaged in conversations with Europeans; inevitably they would ask what I was doing here, something that was hard enough to explain to myself. Nevertheless, I walked across to speak to them.

They were Swiss, charming and interesting. Jean Ziegler was Professor of Sociology and Third World Studies at Geneva University, and the UN's recently appointed Special Rapporteur on 'The Right to Food'; Erica Deuber-Ziegler was a renowned medieval art historian. Over coffee and a bottle of water we chatted for a couple of hours, and I heard how they came to be in Djanet. Through his position at Geneva University Jean Ziegler had at one time and another developed close affinities with and high-level contacts in Algeria. In recognition of his interest in the country, he had been invited to chair a symposium in Algiers and then to enjoy a holiday as a guest of the government. The problem was, as Jean explained to me, that they were getting the red-carpet treatment wherever they went, and finding it quite impossible to travel and see the people of the country as they would otherwise have wished.

'We've just escaped from our minders!' Jean said when I asked him what he was doing in the street café without a bodyguard. 'But we have to be back at the Mayor's residence soon. There is a reception for us, and then we're catching tonight's flight to Tamanrasset.' They were pleased to find I was headed there on the same flight. They wanted to meet local Tuareg and, should it prove possible, were keen to join me on my own strange journey, if only for a day or two. The idea of their company was immensely attractive, and I knew that they would find a warm welcome among the Tuareg; they were that sort of people. We agreed to get together on the plane and make plans.

By the time Abdel Khader drove me out to the airport it was raining heavily, closer to the scarp almost torrentially.

'Is the *oued* flowing yet?' I asked him.

'Another hour or two – perhaps by midnight,' he replied. 'Then it will be running strong.'

Later, as I sat at the airport waiting for my flight, a policeman who had just driven out from Djanet confirmed that the *oued* was in full flood. I thought of the tons of garbage now on their way to the once pristine desert.

The sign over the exit door of the only waiting-room at Djanet's tiny airport reads 'Gate 24', but one should not be deceived by this into worrying about the mischance of boarding the wrong flight: very few come to this remote corner of the Sahara each week. And the official schedule, no doubt printed out months in advance, must be treated with a little caution. The problem is not that flights are invariably late, which would be quite understandable in this part of the world, but that occasionally they are early. Bahedi had warned me about this possibility. 'The trouble is,' he laughed, 'that when they do arrive early, they are also likely to leave early. It sorts out the over-booking problem!' (It strikes me that there is a strong kinship between Air Algérie jokes and Aeroflot jokes, but having flown with both I think I would give Air Algérie the preference. Its pilots are well trained, and there is a better chance of a crash actually being reported.) To allow for this particular vagary, Abdel Khader dropped me off at the airport with an hour or more in hand, which also gave me an opportunity to finish reading David Lodge's *Changing Places*.

The flight was more or less on time, but clearly overbooked, and this threw a spanner into the almost paranoid security system as prospective passengers identified their luggage out on the air strip as required, but with no certainty of getting a seat. The problem was resolved quite simply, under the time-honoured rubric 'those that are last shall be First'. It began with me, probably because I was the only 'tourist' on the plane. I was asked to vacate my seat (by the emergency exit) and move to First Class, which was empty. Once the steward had directed me to the window seat in the third of the three first-class rows, the 'last' were ushered in. I had a good look at them: they were clearly all locals, and most appeared to be Tuareg. As soon as they had stowed all their plastic bags and other bits and pieces in the overhead lockers and seated themselves the steward pulled the curtain across the cabin, setting us truly apart from *hoi polloi* behind. In all the anxious bustle I had temporarily forgotten about the Zieglers. But I hadn't noticed the two unfilled seats in the front row, and just before the front cabin door was closed, the Zieglers were ushered onto the plane and into their seats. There was only time for a quick mutual acknowledgement before seat belts were fastened and the plane took off. It struck me as entirely fitting that a dozen Tuareg and two professors of sociology should fill the first-class cabin of a plane flying over Ahaggar.

And it was that title 'professor' that was the cause of the trouble that lay in store for us when we arrived at Tamanrasset at three in the morning in a blisteringly cold wind, though it was not until afterwards, when I was sitting outside the airport with Bahedi in his Land Cruiser, that I was able to put two and two together and work out exactly what had just happened on the airstrip.

Bahedi had driven out to the airport an hour or so before the plane was due. A large contingent of officialdom soon arrived – the *Wali* (the head of the regional government), the *Chef du Daira* (the mayor), senior military personages, and just about every other Tom, Dick and Harry of any local civic or military importance. None of these people knew what the important visiting luminary they were there to welcome looked like, so Bahedi had gathered, and few even knew his name; what they did know was that he was a 'professor', and that he was Swiss. Most of them also knew Bahedi, and knew his wife was

Swiss, so it was assumed that he too was at the airport to pay his respects to the visitor. Bahedi, who at this stage knew nothing of Professor Ziegler, unwittingly confirmed this misapprehension: when one of the official welcoming party asked if he was there to meet the 'professor', he answered 'Yes'.

Jean Ziegler can surely have had no premonition of the results of his action, but I do remember that he ushered me out of the plane in front of him. At the time, I put it down to his charming manners. The result, of course, was that I stepped gaily out across the runway towards the waiting crowd some little way ahead of him. Bahedi, seeing me, came forward to greet me, and that was enough for the official party. Secure, as they thought, in Bahedi's identification of the 'Swiss professor', they surged forward in their turn. Briefly I was the focus of much bowing and scraping, my hand was shaken most deferentially and I was asked if I had had a good flight. Yes, indeed I had, and I thanked them very much for their concern. Did I have a fleeting vision of being hailed by the Algerian government as the saviour of thirteen thousand years of rock art, this reception just the first of many? In truth, I knew almost at once that I was in the midst of a farce which would do me no good at all.

Subsequent events are rather muddled in my mind, for everything seemed to happen rather quickly. At one point I swear I saw Jean and Erica making a beeline for the airport building, but in fact I think Jean realised at once that he had inadvertently landed me in a situation from which I needed rescuing. Bahedi, with true Tuareg humour, later admitted that he couldn't think why the top brass should be laying out the red carpet for me! Fortunately, both Jean and Bahedi got to my side at about the same time. Jean's smile was mischievous, as if to intimate that he had *almost* succeeded in getting away. I tried to make a sort of introduction–cum–apology to the Wali, but fear it must have sounded rather frivolous. Then, clutching Bahedi's arm, I sidled away as quickly as possible into the enveloping darkness. The last I saw of Jean – we never got those plans for a joint trek made – was his hand on his head, trying to control long wisps of hair in the wind as he was escorted into the airport's *Salle d'honneur*.

9

Tourha

the one that got away

AFTER A LONG sleep and another hot shower, I spent the rest of my first day back in Tamanrasset with Bahedi and Claudia, discussing what to do about the Jabbaren theft. I needed to know more about the extent of the damage to rock art in Ahaggar. Was the theft at Jabbaren an isolated case? Had I missed other such thefts in the area? Was the vandalism I had seen in the Tassili restricted to the Djanet region, or did it extend to more remote sites in other parts of the Tassili? Indeed, were there any sites either still undiscovered, or completely untouched and undamaged by tourists and antiquity-hunters?

The more we asked questions, the more we became aware of the dearth of answers. So it was that we decided to turn the whole problem around, and start by exploring the least-known and most remote parts of the region. Our first selection almost chose itself, a region known as Ahellakane. Neither Bahedi nor I had ever been there, although we had both been close to it at different times. Ahellakane is part of the Tassili-n-Ajjer mountains, five or six hundred kilometres north of Tamanrasset, and to the immediate east of the Amguid gorge. As for as we knew, this part of the Tassili was relatively unexplored and uninhabited, except for a few nomadic Tuareg who possibly still sometimes moved their herds into the region.

Our second selection was the broken ring of heavily eroded mountains in the extreme south-west of Ahaggar, the Tassili-ta-n Tin

Ghergoh and the Tassili-ta-n Tin Massao, three or four hundred kilometres from Tamanrasset and not far from the Niger and Mali borders. This was an area that we knew to be politically sensitive because of the movements of *contrabandiers* and 'bandits' crossing into Algeria from the south, so we weren't sure if we would be allowed to travel there. We decided to explore Ahellakane first.

For safety reasons, we would need two vehicles. Bahedi made all the arrangements while I agreed to cover the cost of all fuel, food and other supplies as well as paying the drivers, guides and anyone else we might need. Hosseyni wasn't able to come with us, so Bahedi asked another friend, Nagim, who had his own Toyota Land Cruiser, to join us. When I first met Nagim he was fully veiled, with a fierce, almost film-star look to him; unveiled he appeared more ordinary, but proved to possess good humour and a great sense of fun. Hamed, who often drove for Bahedi, was to take charge of the second Land Cruiser, while Moustaffa, who normally looked after the *gîte* complex, was in charge of food supplies and cooking.

Arranging for the vehicles and supplies was the easy part. We still had to find guides who knew Ahellakane. Bahedi made enquiries and soon heard that Agag was in Tamanrasset. Agag was an old man of the Ait Lowayen Kel Tourha, and a distant cousin of Mokhtar. We found him easily, and discovered that his brother Hamdi, who was camped at the southern end of the Tourha mountains, knew the Kel Tourha who were camped close to Ahellakane.

It took us less than two days to organise and equip ourselves. As we trundled out of Tamanrasset on the morning of the third day, picking up Agag on the way, we were well laden: fuel for at least sixteen hundred kilometres, eight 25-litre jerricans of water, cooking utensils and food supplies for at least seven people for seven to ten days, three spare tyres, and everyone's bedding and other personal belongings.

The immediate plan was to drive north up the main tarmac road and then turn east to the village of Ideles, two hundred-odd kilometres from Tamanrasset. If we were lucky we might find diesel fuel there, enabling us to top up and give ourselves a further safety margin. From Ideles, Agag would take us to Hamdi's camp. He, we hoped, would be able to come with us in his turn and lead us to the few Kel Tourha Tuareg who knew Ahellakane. I had a feeling we might finish up with a lot of Tuareg on board!

We hadn't gone far beyond the airport turn-off, a section of road with which I was now very familiar, when we came across seven or eight gargantuan desert transporters and fuel tankers parked on the side of the highway, all heading towards Tamanrasset.

'What on earth are they doing?' I asked as we drove past.

'Travelling in convey,' replied Nagim, at the wheel next to me. Bahedi was in the back seat, with Moustaffa, Hamed and Agag in the other Toyota. As he spoke we passed another dozen or so trucks, all rumbling along slowly a little further back from the head of the convoy.

'But why? – and why so many of them?'

'Security,' said Bahedi laconically. He seemed by now to expect me to be *au fait* with everything that was going on in the region. It has never been sensible to drive across the Sahara unaccompanied, and most motorists in any case prefer to make up little convoys of two or three vehicles, for company and general safety. But twenty or so big transporters bunched together in a convoy – that was a different league altogether. There was a short pause, then he said: 'Tamanrasset is a big town. Almost everything comes down from the north: fuel, cement, butane gas, flour – just about everything.'

'But security against what?' I hoped I didn't sound too persistent.

'*Contrabandiers.*'

'Like those that passed Hosseyni near Mertoutek the other week?'

'Yes, probably. Smuggling is big business now. Cigarettes. Maybe other things.'

'But surely smugglers would steer clear of other traffic, and especially the main road?'

'Well, some are also bandits,' said Bahedi.

'What? Like the "men in the mountains" in the north?' I used the accepted colloquialism for the Islamic fundamentalists, still lodged in their bases in the Atlas Mountains, carrying on their war against the government.

'Not quite like those in the north, but they too are against the Algerian state.'

Both Bahedi and Nagim seemed reluctant to answer my questions, except in the most general way. Suddenly, getting information out of either one was like drawing teeth. It was like trying to make a Sicilian violate his duty of *omerta* to the Mafia, just as when I had tried to raise the subject in the Tefedest. But I sensed I was inching closer to understanding much that had been perplexing me – the multitude of tracks across the desert that seemed to go nowhere, the vehicles that passed Hosseyni without stopping, the hyper-active security I'd noticed first at In Salah and then personally experienced when boarding planes at both Tamanrasset and Djanet – and the helicopter gunships I had seen parked on the apron at Tamanrasset's airport. And presumably all these straws in the wind were connected with the 'incidents in the south-east of the country' referred to in the Foreign Office reports. I sensed chinks in the wall of silence; if I could keep the conversation going ... 'People like Hadj Bettu?' I hadn't got far with that name the last time, but it was worth another try.

'Not Bettu,' said Bahedi, as he had once before, 'but people like that.'

'You mean, people down here in the south?' I asked.

I'd scarcely dared hope it would work, but the implication that Tuareg were involved proved to be the key that unlocked the silence. Bahedi's immediate response was: 'Oh no, not people from here – from the north, but operating from down here, from over the border in Niger and Mali.'

'Not Tuareg, then?' It was pretty certain that Algeria's Tuareg, the Kel Ahaggar, would hesitate to get involved in any serious action against the government, but I was by no means so sure about Tuareg in Niger and Mali, where the Tuareg uprisings in the 1980s and early 1990s were still part of recent memory.

'No, not Tuareg, although there may be some down south who are involved. He's a Chaamba, from Metlilli.' I noted the reference to 'he' – one man.

'What's his name?'

'Mokhtar.'

'Like you,' I said, trying to keep things light. 'It seems that almost everyone I have come across on this trip is called Mokhtar.'

'And it's not a very common name, either,' said Bahedi. 'He's Mokhtar ben Mokhtar.'

'And a Chaamba.' The Chaamba are traditional enemies of the Tuareg.

'But he probably has many different names. And – who knows? – – maybe he's just a myth, and doesn't really exist at all.'

'*Louar*,' said Nagim, who had been driving without saying anything for the last few minutes.

'What's *louar*?' I asked.

'His name — what he's known as. *Le borgne.*' Nagim was speaking French, but could see that I had not understood what he meant. '*Borgne* is French for one-eyed,' he said. 'In Arabic, *louar.*'

Bahedi came to my rescue. 'It's said that he went to fight in Afghanistan and lost an eye there. Apparently he wears a glass eye.'

'Is that true? It certainly makes him *sound* like a bandit! Has anyone ever seen him?'

'I don't know. I don't think so. Well, except for Nagim.'

I wasn't sure if I had heard or understood Bahedi correctly, and turned in my seat to look at him directly. 'Nagim? What do you mean?' As well as surprise, my tone probably reflected a certain amount of anxiety.

'Yes, Nagim was captured by him.'

I couldn't believe what I was hearing. Surely Bahedi was making a joke at my expense?

'Is that true?' I asked Nagim.

'Why, yes. I have even sat in his vehicle with him.' His reply carried a suggestion of indignation at my apparent disbelief.

'How did that come about?'

'I was driving with my wife and three children and stumbled into a convoy he had just held up near Arak.* It was quite funny, really. My youngest child was a baby, and needed a bottle of milk. Mokhtar actually provided the milk, and we sat in the front of his vehicle feeding the baby. He was very charming. He said his fight was against the state, not the people of Algeria.'

Just another Robin Hood, I thought.

I asked Nagim about Mokhtar ben Mokhtar's vehicle. It was what Tuareg referred to as a 'Station', a fast, petrol-driven Toyota pick-up with very wide, soft tyres that enabled it to travel at speed over sandy terrain. 'And on the inside,' said Nagim, 'right across the top of the windscreen, was written *LIBÉRATION DU GRAND SUD.*'

'That's pretty heavy stuff,' I said. 'Does he mean it?'

'Who knows?' said Bahedi. 'As far as the government is concerned, he is at war with Algeria.'

'So that's the reason for the conveys?'

'Yes, but only down to about In Eker,' Nagim answered. 'This section of road is safe. The area that is dangerous is either side of

---

* Arak is the gorge into Ahaggar on the road from In Salah to Tamanrasset.

Arak.' I thought about the geography, and it made sense. If 'One-eye' was based south of the border, between Niger and Mali, he could come up the western side of Ahaggar, keeping well to the west of Tamanrasset, and then turn east and help himself to supplies on the main road around Arak, where the gorges are well-suited to ambush, offering protection and quick escape routes.

'And the government can't catch him?' As I asked it, I realised it was a fairly stupid question.

'Not so far,' Bahedi answered. 'But the problem is that for all we know there are other groups of bandits and *trabandistes* [as the smugglers were called] that may be trying to emulate him – copy-cats. Possibly many things that are ascribed to him are being done by other groups. No one knows. And, of course, stories and myths get about and become exaggerated.'

'What about the *trabandistes*? What are they up to?'

'The big business is cigarettes. The whole country is flooded with them. All the cigarettes on the kiosk stalls in Tamanrasset are contraband. They are mostly Marlboro, Philip Morris. They are made in their factory in northern Nigeria, trucked into Niger and Mali and then transhipped onto the 'Stations' – and *choof* – they travel fast, right across the desert, up into Algeria to intermediaries, and then on up to the north – maybe even across to Europe!'

A lot of those 'straws in the wind' were beginning to make sense, and I even felt a glimmer of sympathy for the Algerian government. On top of all its other problems, it scarcely needed bandits and smugglers riding footloose and fancy free around the Sahara, especially with a desert frontier extending to close on six thousand kilometres. And there were deeper implications, of course: what if these 'bandits', perhaps driven by Louar's crazy notion of some sort of 'free' Saharan State, were linked up with the fundamentalists in the north, supplying them with arms, say, or financing them through smuggled cigarettes? It certainly gave one food for thought.

'It's amazing,' I said, thinking it better to play down what I had heard. 'Quite a business.'

We turned off the main road at the same junction as on my earlier journey to the Tefedest. This time, however, we kept to the *piste* that ran due east through the little village of Hirafok and on to Ideles, our immediate goal that afternoon. We hadn't gone far when we spotted a makeshift camp a little way from the *piste*, and a man waving at us to stop. Ebegui was an Issekemaren Tuareg and wanted a lift to Hirafok, where he lived and where, as he told us, he had a big garden. He climbed aboard, but only a few minutes later pointed out that we had reached a good place to stop for lunch. He was a tall man, and well-fleshed – I suspected that gastronomic interests lay behind his suggestion. It was still quite early, and I don't think anyone else felt like stopping to eat at that stage, but it was somehow impossible to argue with Ebegui: he was too large and too domineering, and much too jovial. Having selected the time and the *oued* in which we were to stop, he also selected the tree under which we would take our midday rest. Rather like himself, it was an imposing tree in all respects – tall, well-crowned, and leafy enough to afford good shade – but hornets had already made their nest in it. They too were huge, with broad yellow and black stripes, at least twice the size of English hornets, and they took exception to Ebegui's sweeping of the ground under the tree to clear it of thorns so that we could enjoy its shade. We tried to settle down on the carpets, but the hornets zoomed about, as much incensed by our presence as they were attracted by our food. Neither Ebegui nor Agag was bothered by them in the slightest, which was reassuring, and Moustaffa and Hamed were too busy with preparations for lunch to notice them. But I could see that both Bahedi and Nagim were ill-at-ease, as I was.

'Aren't they dangerous?' I asked Bahedi.

'Only when they are upset,' answered Ebegui, who had overheard me.

I don't know what more we could have done to upset them: seven humans had come crashing into their domain, cleared the ground, lit a fire, and proceeded to swat them, and he assumed that they weren't upset. On the other hand, no one was stung.

Moustaffa prepared an excellent lunch of fresh lettuce salad, with tinned tuna, fresh tomatoes, onions, sliced cucumber and olives, and the fresh bread we had collected from the bakery on our way out of Tamanrasset. Ebegui ate his fill and dominated the conversation, Agag his main audience. Bahedi and Nagim said very little. When there was a lull in the near-monologue I asked – as only a foreigner could be excused for doing, since it was so impolite – whether it was true that the Isekkemaren were now the richest of all the Kel Ahaggar tribes in terms of camels, something Bahedi had told me on the way back from the Tefedest. Crossing this part of Ahaggar not far from where we were now, we had counted more than eighty camels and about a dozen Isekkemaren tents set back about a mile from the *piste*. In earlier times one always thought of the noble Kel Rela or some of the stronger Kel Ulli vassal tribes as having the most camels. But now things had changed: the Isekkemaren had clung persistently to the nomadic way of life, and rather specialised in camels, so that what Bahedi said was probably true. Ebegui could scarcely confirm it, of course, for fear of the misfortunes of the evil eye. He had no choice but to answer me with denials, while everyone else laughed at his slight unease. Soon afterwards we left: the hornets made a siesta quite impossible. Ebegui's bonhomie was amusing but somewhat exhausting, and I think we were all relieved when we finally dropped him off in Hirafok.

As we drove through the dusty little village, a man with a beaming face came running towards us from one of the mud-brick houses, arms waving, veil falling down all over the place. He peered through the window to greet us.

'You remember him?' Bahedi asked.

'Yes,' I said. 'I know that face, but I can't place him.' As I spoke, it came back to me. How could I have forgotten a name like Fenu Fenu? Bahedi had introduced us in Tamanrasset before we set out for the Tefedest. He had hoped to come with us, but was too tied up with some sort of business.

'How did he ever get a name like that?' I had asked

'I don't know. He was an old Dag Rali slave and always made people laugh, so he just started calling himself Fenu Fenu. I think he just liked the name, and that was that. So now he's Fenu Fenu!'

'Just saying the name wants to make you laugh.'

'I know. That's probably why he took it.' As we drove off, I waved back at Fenu Fenu. I don't think I have ever seen a face that could make one feel happier; and yet, for these people, there wasn't so much to laugh about.

I have never much liked this part of Ahaggar, from the main road through Hirafok and on to Ideles. I have walked it so many times, both alone and on camel, and perhaps it's to do with bad memories.

But really, I think, it's because it is rather bland. The Tuareg call it Arechchoum, the meaning of which has never been made clear to me. It is not a plain, although most of it is pretty flat, but nor is it a valley – it's just rather amorphous. Bounded by the high mountains of Atakor some eighty or so kilometres to the south and by the southern end of the Tefedest range about the same distance away to the north, much of it is covered in barren, stony lava cut through by hundreds of almost insignificant little valleys containing a few stunted thorn bushes and scrappy, desiccated pasture. Good water lies not far below the surface, however, hence the abundant wells and gardens at Hirafok, where the water table is only a few metres below the surface of the *oued*; indeed, it is the rainwater draining off the northern slopes of Atakor and down into Arechchoum that is now pumped up and piped to Tamanrasset. One can see the route of the pipe, buried just below the surface alongside the main road to Tamanrasset. Big taps have been inserted at intervals so that nomads can water their herds.

We reached Ideles at about four in the afternoon, to find the village looking surprisingly empty. Crossing over the *oued*, we turned left in the direction of the school and most of the other main buildings, and then right onto the long, dusty dirt road that heads out of town, ostensibly to nowhere. It looked more like a stage prop for some latter-day Western than a village in the Sahara. Like most of the surrounding hills and plain, the surface of the street was a blackish-grey colour, testament to the volcanic origins of the area and the consequent richness of the soil. It was here at Ideles, around 1840, that Tuareg first attempted agriculture in Ahaggar, using their slaves.

The street was wide, like a street in a Western, and for part of its length could even be described as dual-carriageway. Broken kerbstones and the remains of a pavement extended intermittently for part of its length. But its most memorable feature was it street lights. I don't think a single lamppost stood truly erect: almost every one was either bent, as if a vehicle had driven into it – unlikely, since scarcely any pass along this street – or tilted to one side or the other. They looked like a line of drunks. The tops of the lampposts were elegantly curved to support large, tulip-shaped glass shades, irresistibly reminiscent of the promenade of a North Wales seaside resort when Art Nouveau was in fashion, except that most of them, even on the more upright posts, were smashed, leaving jagged shards of glass sticking out of the sockets. How they got to Ideles defies imagination; the Sahara is full of such incongruities.

We stopped just before the last lamppost on the way out of town. Ahead of us, the *piste* snaked on across a stony plain towards a low line of rocky hills in the distance. I might have said 'snaked on into empty desert' – but one thing about the Sahara, and especially Ahaggar, is that very little of it is truly 'empty'. On our right, and the reason why we had stopped here, were two pumps, one for diesel and one for petrol. Both had the appearance of having been disembowelled, and I could not believe they worked. The attendant was supposed to come on duty at five, still half an hour away; the general dearth of other vehicles didn't encourage us to think punctuality would be his strong point. We sat about on the broken bits of pavement by the pumps, and waited.

Opposite the pumps was the *gendarmerie*, the very last building on the way out of town. It had a rather 'French' look to it. Bahedi decided that it would be wise to show them our papers, largely as a safety precaution: we really were going off the beaten track, into what could almost be called 'unexplored territory'. He returned within five minutes, confirming that everything was in order, only for a *gendarme* to appear a short while later and demand that I accompany him to the *gendarmerie*, on my own and with my passport. Bahedi was most upset. The *gendarmes* had no right to harass tourists in this way, he said, and insisted on coming with me. I thought it wiser not, for I could see he was getting a bit hot under the collar, and tried to calm him down. They were only young men from the north, I told him, bored out of their minds. Probably they had never seen a foreign passport in their lives, certainly not here in this far-off Saharan outpost. 'If I'm not back in ten minutes, come and rescue me!' I said gaily, and left him standing by the Land Cruisers and looking distinctly irritated.

There were four young *gendarmes* in the station, all wearing track-suits and trainers. It was clear that, as I had suspected, they had absolutely nothing to do but kill time. All four went to the other side of a high, empty counter and searched underneath it for something which turned out, when found, to be a tatty exercise book with French-style squared paper evidently serving as some sort of station log-book. The one who had asked for my passport – he was presumably the 'duty officer', the most senior or, more likely, the most literate – took charge and opened the exercise book. When he saw me looking at it – I couldn't see anything written in it – he told me to sit down on my side of the counter. I pulled the one chair available up to the counter and duly sat on it, which of course made conversation difficult because my head was now below the counter and we could not see each other.

So many problems! First of all he couldn't find my details in my passport, entirely the fault of whoever designed the new EU passports with all the relevant bits at the end. 'Towards the back,' I said, peering over the counter as he flicked back and forth through the passport. Eventually he found the details, in English and French. Another problem: he spoke good French, but could only read and write Arabic. Standing up, I asked if I could help, and he didn't object. We made good progress through name, nationality, passport number, date of birth, and sex, but then got bogged down over my place of birth. 'Crediton,' I said, and watched as he carefully wrote it into the exercise book in Arabic, wondering idly if Crediton had ever been transliterated into Arabic before. 'And where is that?' he asked. I had almost said 'Devon' when I realised that would make things even more complicated. 'In England,' I said instead, and added: 'It's just a little village, not much bigger than Ideles.' That put an end to his interest in Crediton. For a man from the north, Ideles must seem like the ends of the earth.

I thought that was it: he had filled up the best side of a page in the exercise book, and I had been polite and helpful. Then he found my visa, and decided that should also be copied into the exercise book. Happily it had an Arabic transliteration alongside the French, which meant that he could rattle through it: visa number, passport number, number of entries, length of stay, reason for journey, place of issue. But that was not the end. He wanted the name of my father. 'That's not required to be given either in my passport or on the visa,' I said, in a friendly tone. 'Anyhow, he's dead. He's been dead for fifty-six years, killed in the war, before I was born.' I thought this bit of family history might touch a chord. Over a million Algerians had been killed in their War of Independence, leaving many young men of his age without fathers.

He wasn't moved. '*I* need it,' he said, as if that explained everything.

'The same as mine,' I said. 'Keenan.' He wrote down 'Keenan' for the third time, in Arabic.

'And the first name?'

'Hugh,' I said. I thought the transliteration might present difficulties, but he managed.

'And your mother's name?'

Normally I would by now have been seething. All this was quite unauthorised, and everything necessary was on the official police documentation Bahedi had given the *gendarme* at the outset. But we had time on our hands and I was curious to know how many more questions he could dream up. There were still my wife and children to be worked through. 'There's a bit of a problem with my mother's name,' I said. 'She's got seven. Would you like them all?'

'One will do.' His tone was dead-pan, and he did not look up.

Which one, I wondered, would look best in the exercise book?

'Fleischman,' I decided, and watched as it was transliterated.

With this he seemed satisfied, and made to get up and close the book.

'You've missed one thing,' I said.

'What's that?'

Leaning over, I reopened my passport at the visa page and pointed to where it said '*Taxe Perçue 200DA*'.

'You should note down that it cost two hundred dinars!' It was risky: if someone has no sense of humour, there's little point in trying to be funny.

'Can you believe it?' said a voice behind me, convulsed with laughter. 'He paid two hundred dinars to come here!' I hadn't noticed Bahedi come in; his sense of humour was robust. 'You really should write that down,' he said.

'Everything's fine,' I said quickly to Bahedi, trying to turn him around and usher him towards the entrance. It looked as though the *gendarme* was going to react in all the wrong ways. 'We were just having a chat. I'll see you at the car in a minute.'

Bahedi went outside, and I spent a few minutes saying goodbye to the *gendarmes*, telling them I would see them again in a week or so if we came back this way.

'Not me,' said one. 'I'm leaving tomorrow.'

'Going home?'

'Yes. Tomorrow.' He could not disguise his excitement.

'Where is home?' I asked. But I didn't recognise the name he mentioned. 'Where is that?' I had to enquire.

'Near Relizane.'

There had been a lot of killing in that area over the last few years.

'Take care,' I said. 'It sounds as if they need you more there than here.' Which might or might not be true, bearing in mind all I had heard about 'One-eye'. 'Have a good journey,' I was tempted to add, 'and don't let Louar steal your trousers!' But I doubted very much whether my humour would be appreciated. The tittle-tattle going around was that whenever Mokhtar ben Mokhtar happened to encounter and capture patrols of *gendarmes* or military, he did not kill them, but took them to within walking distance of safety, stripped them to their underpants and sent them on their way.

I left the *gendarmerie* feeling immensely sorry for those four young men. No older than my own son, here they were, stationed for two or three years some two thousand kilometres away from their homes in the north of the country where another 'war' was being fought, in a region and an environment for which they had little affection and, if it were possible, less understanding. Tuareg tended to ridicule them, as they did the army, for their lack of knowledge of the desert, and yet they were the front line against the smugglers and, it seemed from all I'd heard, in an almost secret war against bandits being played out in the middle of the Sahara like a game of fast-moving chess. Furthermore, if we were to come to grief somewhere out there in the desert, these were the young men who would be sent to find us.

I joined the others outside. The pump attendant had been reasonably punctual, the pumps (amazingly) *did* work, and the tanks had been topped up with diesel. Off we set in the late afternoon sun into what was, to all intents and purposes, the great unknown. That evening we would drive as far as Agag's camp, where we hoped to find his brother Hamdi. Before Ahellakane we were going to a place called Tamdjert, more than three hundred kilometres to the north-north-east of Ideles, a journey that would take us through the Tourha mountains, across the great plain of Amadror, around and behind the sand sea of Tihodaine, and up once more onto the Tassili.

I was the only one of us who had ever been to Tamdjert, and I had a very specific reason for wanting to return now. In 1969 I had thought it must be the most isolated, remote and unknown settlement in the whole of Algeria, possibly in the whole Sahara. It was a tiny village of between a hundred and two hundred Kel In Tunin Tuareg, located in a basin about five or six kilometres in diameter right in the centre of the Tassili, about half-way between Djanet in the south-east and Amguid in the north-west, and about half-way across the plateau. The map now shows a *piste* entering the Tamdjert basin. Thirty years ago two French geologists had dropped me off below the Tassili scarp, arranged a rendezvous for three days later, and left me to walk thirty-odd kilometres to find Tamdjert. After a breath-taking walk across the plateau I had explored the basin and the gorges entering it and found the most exquisite rock paintings in caves within the gorges. I now wanted to see if they had been damaged in the intervening years. If the destruction had reached this remote place, then the problem of the Tassili's prehistoric rock art was serious indeed. Tamdjert, as I explained to Bahedi, would be like a litmus test.

As we headed out of Ideles towards Agag's camp, Bahedi was still inclined to complain about the *gendarmes*.

'They shouldn't behave like that. It is quite unnecessary. Can you imagine what it would be like if I had a whole group of tourists, who had paid a lot of money? They wouldn't put up with that sort of non-sense.' He was quite right, of course.

'They're just bored,' I suggested, 'and have nothing else to do.'

Although Agag's camp was only eighteen kilometres from Ideles, it took us an hour to reach it. For the first few kilometres out of Ideles the *piste* was quite reasonable, but the low, rocky hills I had seen from the edge of town turned out to be an almost impassable lava flow. The *piste*, such as it was, had been almost entirely washed away in several places, and because there was so little motorised traffic between Ideles and Djanet, nearly five hundred kilometres away, it had not been repaired. We could only put the vehicles into four-wheel-drive and ease them oh! so slowly over the chaotic piles of rock. It was tedious going, but made bearable for me at least by the stunning views. From the crest of the ridge, the black volcanic rock fell away in front of us over a distance of about five kilometres. Here and there one could just make out sections of the *piste* that had not been washed away. The slope ran down in a big valley full of tamarisk trees and sand that shone brightly in the last of the sunlight. Beyond the valley, the mountains of bare rock rose up again, their harshness now softened as the westering sun picked out one sand-filled valley after another. Further away again I could see the mountains around Tazerouk and, on the horizon itself, the summit of Mount Serkout rising up to more than two and a half thousand metres. I couldn't remember ever being able to see so far or so clearly across this eastern side of Ahaggar before.

Agag's camp was set back on the bank, safe from any possible flood, a few kilometres down the tamarisk-shrouded valley we had been looking into for at least half an hour as we crept down the lava-strewn slopes above it. We stopped the Toyotas and made our own camp amid the tamarisk trees in the middle of the sandy *oued* a little way from Agag's. His younger brother Hamdi was not there. According to Agag's family, he had moved his camp some distance deeper into the Tourha mountains.

We found him early the next morning. Hamdi, I thought, had style. He was of medium height, but slim, which made him appear taller than he was. He wore a traditional indigo-blue veil, and I had a brief glimpse of his face while he was rearranging it. His looks were the nearest I have ever seen to the stereotyped Encyclopedia pictures of Stone-age Man. There was no demarcation between the hair of his head and the beard of his face: both were long, black, curly and unkempt, covering his entire head except for a small area around his eyes, which were equally dark. I would not have liked to do battle with Hamdi. He had had no notice of our coming, and was no doubt surprised to see the two Land Cruisers bearing down on his camp, but he gave no sign of surprise: vehicles seeking out his camp to ask for his services might have been an everyday occurrence.

Agag told him our plans, and he had no objection to coming with us straight away. It was, after all, an opportunity to do what Tuareg enjoy most – travelling through their vast country and visiting distant kinsmen. Bahedi confirmed that we would be paying him the full rate for a 'special guide', his task being to accompany us to Tamdjert and then to help us find a route into Ahellakane. His only conditions were that before setting off we should drive to the camp of one of his kinsmen a couple of valleys deeper into the Tourha, to collect some *udi*, soured goat's butter and a favourite relish of the Tuareg (without which, clearly, he would have been a bad travelling companion), and then track down his wife, who was with the goat herd, so that he could tell her what he was doing.

Hamdi's camp seemed to reflect his own strong presence. It was pitched on a slight bluff on the outer bank of a wide sweep of valley that reminded me of a place I had once seen in Montana. The surrounding mountains had a certain strength to them, not in their height, certainly not in their ruggedness, for the mountains of the Tourha have a curious softness to them, but in the way in which they seemed to command the valley. It was obvious why Hamdi had pitched his camp in this valley: it contained some of the best pasture I had seen on this trip.

It took less than five minutes for Hamdi to collect his personal belongings, a pile of blankets into which were wrapped what looked like a spare *gandoura* and a few other accoutrements, and climb aboard. We were now seven.

It took another half-hour to reach the kinsman's camp and collect the small bottle of *udi*. The way in which *udi* is made differs very slightly, so I am told, between various northern and southern Tuareg. Basically, the morning yield of goat's milk is put into a skin bag and left to sour until the following morning. In the heat of summer the bag will be left in the shade of the tent, in winter placed in the sun or close to the fire. After souring it is churned, usually in a camel-skin bag, and then heated, traditionally in an earthenware pot. Some Tuareg add parts of certain plants to flavour the butter, others sometimes add a meal made from dried dates. In the past, some Tuareg say, ground *mouflon* horn would sometimes be added. *Udi* is dark yellow in colour and has a strong flavour – a teaspoonful or two is enough to flavour a large dish of food. Tuareg love it and will add it to almost every dish, especially the bread or *tagella* which now forms the staple diet of most nomads. Foreigners often find it unpleasant at first, but it is a readily acquired taste.

With the *udi* stowed safely on board we had merely to find Hamdi's wife, and this we could do on our way as she had taken the herd in that direction. We stopped a short distance from the nearest goats, which had spread out across a wide valley almost as well pastured as the ones in which Hamdi and his kinsmen were camped. There had obviously been some good rain in this part of Tourha recently, which would also account for the relative abundance of *udi*. We sat and watched as Hamdi picked his way around the clumps of yellowy-green grass across the flat valley floor towards his wife. They were too far away for me to see whether they touched, but they walked close together, slowly and in step, for at least ten minutes. We started up the Toyotas and followed them. The early morning sun slanting into the valley highlighted the blue, black and cerise of their robes. There was a timeless quality to the picture they made, the rough-looking man in his forties, one of the Sahara's last genuine nomads, walking alone with his wife in this serene valley, far from the pace and pressures of the modern world.

Hamdi, as 'special guide', rode in the lead vehicle with Agag, Moustaffa and Hamed. Bahedi, Nagim and I followed on behind. Hamdi would not have any 'guiding' to do until Ahellakane, as the way across the vast plain of Amadror presented few difficulties: you just followed the tracks, or took the direction from the sun or a compass, until you picked up the landmarks you knew on the other side; if you knew the area well, you could get your bearings from the few isolated hills and ridges that stick out of the plain here and there. The trouble with following another vehicle in the desert is dust: invariably you are driving in its wake. Nagim, who was at the wheel, tended to hang back a good distance, which also gave him a better chance to spot any gazelles the lead vehicle might flush out.

It was still more than three hundred kilometres to Tamdjert, and I doubted that we would get there by nightfall, as we had planned. I soon had a sense that Hamdi was leading us in entirely the wrong direction. 'Aren't we off-course?' I asked Bahedi, wondering if I had momentarily lost my bearings.

'He knows that we are looking for cave paintings. I guess he's taking us to the ones around here that he mentioned to me when we were leaving his camp.' Sure enough, Hamdi took us into another valley where at the base of a broken cliff face were a couple of small caves. The paintings inside were comparatively recent and of little significance or interest, but Hamdi had established his credentials.

The next distraction was soon upon us. We were in the last foot-hills of the Tourha mountains, just before they melt into the vast, flat plain of Amadror, when Nagim's sharp eyes spotted three *mouflon* crossing a sandy plain between two of the hills. Without peer for speed and agility amid rocky mountain peaks and crags, on sand the *mouflon*'s sharp, narrow hooves serve him ill. Nagim's eyes lit up, the engine raced, and the Land Cruiser immediately tore off in deter-mined pursuit. The *mouflon* were still some distance from the safety of the mountains, and Nagim knew he was in with a chance. We careered across the desert surface, bouncing over the almost imperceptible dried-up rivulet beds that contoured the ground and lurching through hidden patches of soft sand. For ten minutes or so the odds were even as the three, led by a large, very shaggy old 'grandfather', struggled through the uncertain sandy footing towards the mountains. *Mouflon* are always vulnerable in such open terrain, but I had a feeling the big fellow had just a little extra in hand. As we reached the stony lower slopes of the mountains, he was less than a hundred metres ahead of us – the other two had veered away and were now safe. Crashing through the gears, Nagim sent the Toyota hurtling up the rocky slope, oblivious alike, it seemed, of danger to us or damage to the vehicle.

At about fifty metres from the *mouflon*, Nagim realised he could motor no further. Opening his door and grabbing his club, kept attached to the gear-stick against just such an eventuality, he hurled himself like a man demented towards the big *mouflon*. Apparently now assured of his own safety, the *mouflon* stopped for a moment on the crest of the hill to take one last, arrogant look at Nagim, who by this time was himself on all fours, having slipped as he threw his club in one last desperate effort to secure his prey.

There was uproar in the Toyota, as Bahedi and I alternately cheered on the *mouflon* and laughed at Nagim's antics. Both of us, I know, were on the *mouflon*'s side, but we had to show support for our hero. When we had all calmed down and Nagim was dusting himself off, Bahedi said to me, almost apologetically, 'I'm not so fond of hunting, you know.'

'One for the pot is fine,' I replied diplomatically. I had never met a Tuareg who was not driven to superhuman endeavours if it came to the chance of bagging a gazelle or, better still, a *mouflon*.

The other four had also been watching Nagim's demonstration of his skills, and as the day wore on the perspective on the morning's events shifted, as is the way with hunting tales. The fact was that Nagim never got closer than about thirty metres to the *mouflon*. He put it at about twenty metres, and no one was disposed to argue with him. By evening, we were all agreed that the great hunter had easily been within touching distance of one of the largest *mouflon* in the area, and that only the steepness of the terrain had saved it. That night, as we sat around our camp fire, Bahedi turned to me and said, quietly, but just loudly enough for the others to hear, 'I remember once hearing a story about a fisherman.'

'Oh, yes?'

'Each time he came home empty-handed, his hands spread further and further apart to describe the huge fish that got away – so much so that the villagers eventually tied his wrists together. The next day he returned and began to describe an absolute monster that had got away. "It sounds as if it must have been enormous," said the villagers mockingly. "Yes, it was," said the fisherman. Then, opening his hands as wide as he could with his tied wrists, he said: "It had eyes this big."' Nagim didn't think the story was very funny.

By midday we had travelled about a third of the way across Amadror and were virtually out of sight of land – crossing Amadror really is like being at sea: flat as far as the eye can see in every direction. The gravel plain slopes imperceptibly northwards for a hundred and fifty kilometres, with scarcely a trace of vegetation, until it becomes submerged under the erg or sand sea of Tihodaine. In Palaeolithic times,* about a quarter of a million years ago, Tihodaine was a great lake whose wooded shores resounded with the cries of both wild animals and Stone Age hunters; Amadror was then a great savannah-covered plain on which those hunters roamed and made their hearths. Beneath the sands of Tihodaine lie the bones of the elephants and many other species of wildlife that once roamed this country and whose remains were washed into the great lake. When the Sahara became more arid and the lake eventually dried up, around 18,000 years ago at the beginning of the last Ice Age, its sediments were whipped up by the wind into the sand sea of today. When the Ice Age retreated five or six thousand years later, the climate of the Sahara again became wetter and Tihodaine may at this time have become lake-like again, the savannah-covered plain of Amadror once more the home of both hunters and pastoralists.

I remember that when I first crossed Amadror some thirty years ago, I was transfixed by the dozens of prehistoric hearths dotting the gravel surface. Stone implements, especially grinding stones and mortars, lay scattered around the hearths, for all the world as though everyone had gone out for a walk after dinner, and never returned. Now I stared out of the window for hours as we drove across that flat gravel wasteland, but didn't see a single implement. It was immensely disappointing, but not surprising. The French set a fashion in collecting such archaeological remains, ostensibly for museums but in reality

---

* Palaeolithic culture in North Africa is known as Acheulean from around 1.7 million to 100–70,000 years ago; Mousterian from around 100,000 to 35,000 years ago; and Arterian from around 40,000 to 20,000 years ago.

mostly as souvenirs and for private collections. And professionals, notably Henri Lhote, who paid Tuareg to collect stone arrowheads and other such artefacts for him, led the way. Almost everyone who has travelled the Sahara has probably picked up and taken away, usually quite innocently, an arrowhead or something similar. And the trend had not abated. It has been estimated that some two million stone artefacts and prehistoric bones have been hoovered up by the French colonialists and the tourists who followed them; it seems doubtful that this figure is as exaggeration. Apart from a couple of broken grinding stones in the bed of the *Oued* Amezzar, in the six days I had spent trekking across the Tassili I had not seen a single prehistoric implement. I was now crossing Amadror; still a natural museum only thirty-five years ago, now it too had been hoovered. Here and there I spotted a few prehistoric camp sites, but there was no trace of those exquisitely honed artefacts Stone Age man left as his legacy. To the untrained eye these sites are now nothing more than little clusters of slightly discoloured stones.

When we stopped to eat and rest for a couple of hours in a shallow *oued* in which three or four spindly acacias offered a choice of shade, I turned up an old grinding stone and a piece of fossilised wood buried in the *oued*'s sandy bed.

Over lunch, I watched and listened as my Tuareg companions excitedly relived the morning's hunt. Perhaps, after all, Neolithic and modern man have a lot in common – though today's technology tilts the odds in favour of the hunter. That said, Nagim had had no luck with a vehicle worth tens of thousands of pounds, and there is something infinitely more beautiful and aesthetically more satisfying about a perfectly crafted Stone Age arrowhead.

10

Amadror
salt mines and prehistoric lakes

SOMEWHERE BETWEEN 'Neolithic Man' and 'Modern Man' lies 'Colonised Man'. In Amadror, the workings of 'colonised man' are found in the salt mines, only a short drive away from where we stopped at midday. The mine – more open cast workings than a mine, in fact – is called Tisemt, the Tuareg word for salt. Rather than take the direct route to Tamdjert diagonally across Amadror we made a slight diversion, keeping to the western side of the plain, so that I could visit Tisemt. I had written about the Saharan salt trade, but had never before had an opportunity to see any of the salt mines.

Tisemt is not easy to find. A person ignorant of the subtle land marks could easily miss it, for it is nothing more than a shallow basin about a kilometre wide and probably no more than seven to ten metres below the surrounding desert surface. On the rare occasions that it rains, a shallow *oued* empties into the basin. I had seen photographs of the workings and heard many a description from Tuareg, but found that neither had captured the essential feeling of Tisemt. It has to be seen: it really is a 'Hell on Earth'. In Russia, it would have been a Gulag, in South Africa, a prison for the opponents of apartheid. In fact, it was probably worse than either; there is absolutely no means of staying alive there.

As we slipped off the gravel plain and drove the short distance across the bed of the *oued* to the edge of the salt workings, conversation gradually died away. It was not conscious. I rather think we all felt a sense of awe. It was as if we were paying our respects to all those who had ever worked and, quite probably, died here. None of my travelling companions had ever worked here; except for Agag and Hamdi, who both claimed to know the area well, they were too young. But we all knew what had taken place here, knowledge and memories which in the case of the Tuareg had been handed down from preceding generations as part of their heritage.

We stopped the vehicles and got out. Even the ground was different, the sand white and crispy, like meringue, because of its salt content. The basin itself looked like an inland lake, its surface broken by choppy brown and white 'waves' up to a metre high. Behind us was a line of isolated tamarisk trees, their trunks now so encased in decomposing old roots and dead branches that they looked more like a line of First World War battleships with big square hulls riding high out of the water and wispy little smoke-stacks on top. It was as if they were trying to steam away from the salt. Beyond them, almost buried in sand, were the scant remains of a few mud-brick walls.

Bahedi saw me looking at the ruined walls. 'That's the remains of the old military post. My father worked here for a couple of years, you know, when he was a *goumier*.'

'Do you know what he did here?'

'Probably just kept an eye on things. There must have been lots of disputes.'

Bahedi and I stayed by the vehicles talking about the history of the place while the others walked across the surface of the salt workings. I could see that it was difficult going. As I discovered when we followed after them, it was like walking over a smashed up ice-floe, the ice being slabs of salt which had broken up and fallen into the old evaporation pits and mine workings, some of which were perhaps a couple of metres deep. One had to watch one's step, for there was scarcely any level surface and it was easy either to slide down a tilted salt 'floe' or to break through the surface and fall into an old hollowed-out working.

It was hot now, almost unbearably so, and I tried to imagine what it must have been like for slaves sent up here to mine the salt in late summer. The temperature in the shade would have been around 45 degrees Celsius, probably nearer 50 (113–122 °F). And there *was* no shade. Nor was there any water other than what they would have carried here in goatskins. As we walked I was surprised by the number of shards of broken pottery and bits of wooden handles scattered about. The pots, I presumed, had been used for storing water, while the wooden handles would have belonged to the hoes and other tools used to cut out the salt.

Over the generations, salt from the Sahara has been carried south-wards in great caravans to the lands along the southern edge of the desert. The mines at Bilma in Chad, at Taoudenni to the north of Timbuktu and here at Amadror were the main sources of that salt, and the starting-points of caravans comprising hundreds, perhaps even thousands, of camels that plodded for weeks on end across the vast expanse of desert. These caravans, as much as the institution of slavery or the fables of *Beau Geste*, are part of the image of the Sahara.

Bahedi and I talked about the history of Amadror's salt trade as we picked our way across Tisemt's crumbling, jagged surface, watching out all the time for our footing. He knew from his father and many others just what it had been like here, while I had read most of the earlier French military and historical reports on the trade.

From the way elder Tuareg talk about the salt caravans, it would be easy to suppose that they had been part of the traditional way of life since the earliest times, yet it was not until 1896 that the first Tuareg carried salt from here to the Sahel. Before then, the salt deposits of Amadror seem not to have been exploited, nor even widely known among the Tuareg. The reason why they began to mine Amadror's salt in that year is closely related to events in Ahaggar and the sur-rounding regions at that time. When drought gripped their country the Kel Ahaggar usually looked to the oases of Touat and Tidikelt to the north of Ahaggar for food, notably cereals and dates. Although the years between 1886 and 1900 seem, on the whole, to have been good for pasture, in 1896 members of two of the strongest vassal Kel Ulli tribes, the Dag Rali and Aguh-en-tehle, carried salt from Amadror to Damergou in Niger, to exchange for millet. And the reason they undertook this first exploratory caravan says much for their initiative, and for their appreciation of the implications of what was happening on the wider stage of the Sahara. The key incident as far as the Tuareg were concerned was that earlier in 1896 the French military had occupied the oases of Tidikelt and Touat, a move which effectively cut the Kel Ahaggar off from a region which was not simply one of their main sources of food supplies, but their ultimate safeguard against the consequences of drought in Ahaggar.

Interestingly, in the wake of the Flatters débâcle of 1881, the French government had calculated that a military occupation of the oases of Touat and Tidikelt would find the Kel Ahaggar's Achilles' heel and cause them 'insuperable difficulties'. And so it proved.

That first caravan appears to have been most successful, but for a number of reasons, mostly political and associated with France's colonial expansion, no further salt caravans travelled to Damergou until 1923, and they did not become an annual event until 1926. From then on the salt caravan became an enormous and almost ritualised undertaking, the central event in the Kel Ahaggar's calendar. Preparations began around August and September, when Kel Ahaggar, or more often their slaves, would trek to Tisemt. Solid bars of salt weighing between fifty and sixty kilos were cut from the deposits and loaded onto camels, two bars on either side, making a total load of up to two hundred and forty kilos. The salt was then taken back to the camps, where the caravans would gradually form, leaving Ahaggar in November or December.

It was a considerable journey, lasting for five to six months and involving, in any one year, anything between two and four thousand camels. From Ahaggar the caravans trekked south for about a month to the plains of Tamesna and the wells of In Abangarit, where they rested for four or five weeks. The camels were turned loose to graze and the weaker ones were replaced by fresh camels from Tamesna for the journey southwards to Tawa and the other markets of Damergou.

When I was learning Tamahak or just chatting with Kel Ahaggar, I often asked them to tell me about the caravans to Niger. The recordings of some of those conversations are almost like music, names of places running off their tongues to the rhythm of the camel's tireless lope, excitement building as the familiar camp sites on the way back north are counted off like the beads on a necklace. 'Six nights from In Abangerit to In Guezzam, off-loading each night to camp at Tin Massao, then the *Oued* Kazourmet, then on to In Seberaka, then Ikadeimellen, Taberok and In Guezzam. And then up to Ahaggar – first to Eradarr, In Teluk – two days at Tagellai, then on to In Attei, Tiouar Tin Zaouaten, Iref In Zedalazen, Tessali, Tigrine, Ain Faig, Tin Adar, Agalella – and then Tamanrasset.'*

---

* This is a literal translation of an old Dag Rali reminiscing about the journey; some of the places are in the wrong order.

Today, Tuareg talk romantically of these caravans, as a thing of the past and as part of their history. In a sense they were romantic. It was a magnificent journey, requiring endurance, discipline, skill and courage. Often, it marked a boy's transition to manhood. But the caravans were hard, and the journey long. Not everyone who left Ahaggar returned. There was always the risk of danger, like that which befell Ihemod ag Ikemma, a Dag Rali and distant kinsman of Khabte. In 1971 I stayed in the camp of his aged widow, Esscbet, who was almost eighty. All but in tears, I listened to her account of what happened:

> He left here with the camels and took Moussa [his son], who was then very young. One morning when they had reached Tamesna, somewhere near In Abangerit, he went off to look for the camels. He told Moussa and Howedi [the son of a slave girl] to stay with the baggage until he returned. He went off – and walked, and walked, and walked a long way looking for the camels until he was tired and had still found nothing. He slept until the next day, and I don't think he could find water. By the evening of the next day he had still not returned. He died there – near a well called Tamer, not far from In Abangerit. I can't remember when it was now – I heard about it when Moussa returned here.

'When was the last caravan?' I asked Bahedi.

He thought for a while. 'Khabte and the others had just come back from a caravan before the trouble at Otoul. When was that?'

'Nineteen-sixty-four,' I said.

'Well,' he considered, 'there were a few after that, although they were intermittent, what with the border closures, and by then they really weren't at all economic. But trade was so bad that they were attractive because they were based on barter – the nomads had no money! And I suppose they were a way of escaping. Independence was still new, and the Government was very repressive.'

'I saw them gathering outside Tamanrasset in the winter of nineteen-sixty-nine,' I said. 'They were waiting for their permits. There weren't very many of them, largely I think because no one seemed to know whether they would be allowed to go.'

'That might well have been the last one. Of course, Kel Ahaggar still keep many of their camels down in Tamesna.'

Talking about those last caravans reminded me of the film I had made of the Tuareg in 1971, and of how Kel Ahaggar were trying to survive in their camps at that time.

'Did I tell you about my stay with Sidi Mohammed ag Ahmadu?'

'Kel Hirafok?'

'That's him, except that he didn't live at Hirafok. He said that he would never leave the mountains.'

'What happened to him?'

It had been another bad year with no rain, and all sixteen of Sidi Mohammed's camels in Ahaggar had died. His whole camp was in a pretty bad state, and by autumn he was insistent that he must make the journey down to Tamesna to get some more camels. He kept saying that he would never leave his 'camp' and the mountains to live in a village, and that he had to have camels. Everyone else, especially the younger men (he was in his mid fifties), kept telling him he was crazy. But he was quite determined.

Sidi Mohammed spent all October and November trying to raise the cash to buy enough grain to maintain his camp during his absence and to hitch a lift south. When he could he even sold off things from his camp to tourists who came to Assekrem. His determination was both tragic and admirable. Nothing was going to stop him. I arrived shortly before his departure, and got the film crew – there were only three of them – to let me use their vehicle to carry his grain back up to the camp. I then drove him back to Tamanrasset to help him get his permit to enter Niger. His twelve-year-old son went with us – it was the first time he had ever been to Tamanrasset. Sidi's wife Umeyda told me that she had gone there once, but hadn't liked it and didn't want to go again.

While I was with Sidi, I tried to get him to explain *why* he needed more camels in the camp, and to consider the expenditure of time and money involved: many of the younger men had told me they thought he was being irresponsible. Sidi just kept on saying that he had 'always' had camels. They were, he insisted, the basis of his wealth and his status. Clearly, for him they were both the symbol and the justification of his 'nomadic' existence. When I asked him how new camels would survive in Ahaggar if the drought continued, he agreed that they too would probably die within a year or two if there was no good rain. I don't know if he was aware how much the younger men, even his closest kin, were beginning to ridicule him. The last I saw of him, he was clutching a camel saddle and a couple of blankets, perched on top of a heavily laden truck as it rumbled south out of Tamanrasset.

'Do you know what happened to him?'

'No, I never saw him again. For me, *he* was the "last caravan" – more a state of mind than anything else.

'After he left we decided to spend some time filming in his encampment, and that provided his family with enough cash and supplies to see them safely through the winter. His was a tragic case. Like Khabte and a few of the other 'old-timers', he was determined not to give in to the modernising forces that were sweeping over the country.'

We had walked almost to the far side of the salt workings, and had caught up with the others. Even at this time of year one was aware of the heat being sucked into the salt and collecting in the old salt vats. In summer it must have been stultifying.

'Does anyone at all come and work here now?' I asked.

'Sometimes a passing truck picks up a load, every now and again. Nothing more.' It was Nagim who replied, and he had picked up a large chunk of salt he planned to take back to Tamanrasset.

I had once tried to calculate how much salt had been taken from Tisemt. On the basis of annual caravans of 2,500 camels for forty years (1926–1966), with one in three or four camels carrying between two hundred and two hundred and fifty kilos of salt, it worked out at about five thousand metric tons.

'That's a huge amount,' said Bahedi. 'A real industry!'

'It certainly was. The only question is whether to thank or blame French colonialism.'

'And the change of diet!' he reminded me. 'When you were here last, you always ate millet in the camps, from Niger. Now it's *tagella*, wheat flour from the north.'

As we drove out of the basin and back onto the flat plain of Amadror, I thought of Bahedi's father working at Tisemt. I could imagine him telling the slaves and their masters jokes and making them laugh while they laboured under the merciless sun. I turned round for one last look. It was only a few hundred metres behind us, but there was absolutely no sign of it.

In front of and to either side there was nothing but flat gravel: not a sign of vegetation or animal life, except for the occasional prints of gazelles and, here and there, the old camel tracks that had been worn into the gravel surface as the beasts trudged their weary way across this forbidding landscape.

We were now heading due east across Amadror, our shadows beginning to stretch forward in front of us. Our landmarks, none of which were yet visible, were the two massifs of Toukmatine and Ounane directly ahead of us, and the sand sea of Tihodaine which would soon be coming up on our left. We would skirt around the southern edge of Tihodaine, then head more or less due north, looking for the route that would take us between the dunes and the foothills of the Tassili up on to the plateau and then, hopefully by nightfall, to the basin of Tamdjert.

We were already running a couple of hours behind time, thanks to Nagim's *mouflon* hunt and spending longer than we had intended at Tisemt. But here on Amadror, with eighty or ninety kilometres of flat gravel in front of us, we could drive fast. Again it seemed that none of us was inclined to talk. It may have mere afternoon somnolence, but I suspect the salt mines have that effect on people.

About half-way across Amadror we came to a slight ridge, an extrusion of lava between two low-lying hills that ran like a spine down the middle of the plain. For nearly ten kilometres we drove slowly, threading our way between the black lava rocks. Once we had crossed the ridge we were back on to flat gravel, and we could see both Toukmatine and Ounane through the haze in front of us, and the dunes of Tihodaine to our left. We drove close to the edge of the sand sea, avoiding the few patches that snaked out onto the gravel like tentacles and one long *seif*-dune that all but linked the sand sea to the mountain of Toukmatine about fifteen kilometres to the south. I remembered a night spent sleeping on the ground there, close to some prehistoric burial mounds, when I was here with the French geologists.

We stuck as close as possible to the edge of Tihodaine, swinging slowly from an easterly to a northerly direction as we rounded the sand sea. It was strange to think that we were driving on what was once the shoreline of a great lake some sixty or more kilometres wide. Even as a sand sea, it looked more beautiful than most lakes. The lowering sun picked out the dunes in all their majestic glory and changing colours, one superimposed on another, rising from the gravel shoreline to a distant and apparently unattainable summit. The ridge of each dune was a fine and flawless line and each sweeping curve unique, more precise, more immaculate and more perfect in form even than the most glorious female body.

Once we had driven around Tihodaine, our route was more uncertain. Of the seven of us, only Hamdi and I had ever been here before. Hamdi seemed pretty confident that he could pick up the route that would take us up onto the plateau, but my memory of the approach was very uncertain. I knew we had to go between the two box-shaped sentinel mountains of Tin Haberti, more than two thousand metres high, on our left, and Ifedaniouene on the right. But that was not all: between the two mountains lay an almost impenetrable mass of moving sand five or six kilometres across. Not only was it all but impassable for vehicles, but it had obliterated whatever tracks might have taken us in the right direction. No wonder, I thought, that the French geologists had left me here to continue my journey on foot. Hamdi, however, knew a passage that outflanked the first main line of sand and enabled us to get in behind the barrier with only a modicum of difficulty in one patch of soft sand, from which we had to dig ourselves out. He also found a short valley full of tamarisk trees, where we stopped to load up with firewood.

For about five kilometres Hamdi then took us on a route running diagonally across a plain of compact sand lying between the sand barrier we had just skirted, the massif of Tin Haberti and the main scarp of the Tassili, over which we now had to find a passage. Hamdi found the route without difficulty. It was extraordinary, probably much like the ramp the Romans built when they finally broke into the Jewish fortress of Masada on the Dead Sea in AD 73, three years after the fall of Jerusalem. I couldn't tell if it had a rock base, but the surface was of compacted sand blown up against the scarp by the wind. It was perhaps a kilometre long, and the incline was low enough for us to attack it at speed. This ramp took us up onto a middle level of the plateau, which though covered in patches of sand had a rocky base that gave the vehicles better purchase, and from which we were able to climb a rocky ascent onto the high plateau. Here the track was not only well defined but, ironically, also well maintained. The map might have been annotated: 'If you can find it, you can drive on it.'

On the way up on to the plateau there were more glimpses of landscape I remembered, but once we were on the summit, many places brought back my earlier journey, especially those at which I had stopped to take photographs. Bahedi, and I think the others, found my story of having once walked into Tamdjert a little incredible. So did I, seeing again the distance and the terrain over which I had travelled. Young and fit, however, in those days I thought nothing of walking eighty kilometres in a day, and the passage from the sand ramp and over the plateau to the basin of Tamdjert was only a little more than thirty.

Darkness had fallen before we reached Tamdjert, so that we had to rely on our headlights in descending the steep track into the basin. It was slow going, and no sooner had we reached the bottom than Hamed inadvertently drove straight into *fesh-fesh*. It had been a long day and we had driven well over three hundred kilometres: we decided to dig ourselves out in the morning.

It was only that night, as I lay in my tent, that my previous visit began to come back to me in detail. When I finally arrived in the basin after my walk across the plateau, the local headman gave me a most hostile reception, demanding to see my papers and telling me I could not stay without permission from the government. Since it was several days' journey over extremely difficult terrain to either Djanet or Illizi and much further to either In Salah or Tamanrasset and since, I gathered, the last vehicle to pass through the basin had been a French military cartographic team, many years earlier, I wondered which government he was referring to.

To my amazement, he produced a battered FLN (Front de Libération National) membership card, and said he had instructions to record and report the details of all strangers entering the area. The way he was carrying on made me wonder whether he knew that Algeria's war of independence had been over for seven years! As we were literally hundreds of kilometres from the nearest tentacle of government authority I was not quite sure how he was going to do his reporting, nor could I imagine where he expected me to go if he didn't allow me to stay here. I had visions of being held captive for several months in this remote settlement while contact was made with the outside world and my release negotiated.

As it happened, I had left all my permits, including my passport, with the French geological team. I wrote my name on the back of a cigarette packet instead, gave it to the headman, and suggested that he take it to Illizi. Then, deciding that caution was the better part of valour, I filled my goatskin water-bag from the *guelta* and made my retreat while the going was good. I had time enough to explore the gorges, but my unexpectedly swift departure from Tamdjert caused me considerable discomfort. I had to spend a couple of nights sleeping out on the plateau and in a shelter near Tin Haberti, and though I had enough water there was little to eat except dried tomatoes and onions until I made contact with the French geologists again.

I never knew for sure why the headman was so belligerent, but suspected it might have had something to do with the fact that the people at Tamdjert were predominantly Kel In Tunin, a descent group who were formerly vassals of the Taitok, the noble tribe expelled by the French from Ahaggar, and whose loyalty was to the chief of the Ahaggar Taitok. After independence he had returned to Ahaggar and been appointed head of the Bureau Politique in Tamanrasset. His name was Ellou ag Amaray, and I imagine he must have been particularly pleased to see the French forced out of Algeria. I went to see Ellou when I eventually got back to Tamanrasset, but he refused to discuss the matter with me; he said the Bureau's affairs were none of my business, and that the Kel Rela (the nobles who had ingratiated themselves with the French and effectively ousted the Taitok) would tell me anything I wanted to know.

I was first up in the morning. I wanted to have a good look at the basin, to see if I recognised it and to get my bearings. I wasn't sure if I could remember exactly where I had found the cave paintings, except that they were on the right-hand side of the gorge coming down from the *gueltas*.

The basin looked much as I remembered it, but I could not see the entrance to the gorge; where I thought it should be there was now a large bank of sand and scrub. I was also a little nonplussed by Hamdi's assertion that there was no *guelta* here, when I had a distinct memory (and photographs) of a series of large rock pools in the gorge.

Before searching for the gorge we drove the few kilometres across the basin to the main village to top up our water supplies from the well. The floor of the basin was just as I remembered it: thousands of small, sandy hillocks no more than a few feet high stabilised by a fairly thick covering of vegetation that provided more or less permanent grazing. The village had grown considerably, and the people were certainly friendlier than on my previous visit. Bahedi and I did a quick hut count and reckoned there must be almost five hundred people living here. We stayed no longer than it took to refill with water, but time enough to discover that the *guelta* was indeed in the gorge, just as I had remembered. We also learned that the old entrance to the gorge was now blocked by sand, so that we would have to enter it from around the back.

Neither the gorge nor the *guelta* was as I had remembered them. Everything seemed to be the wrong way around! I think Bahedi was beginning to wonder if I had brought everyone on a wild goose chase. There was a small settlement near the entrance to the gorge, and we asked there about paintings. One of the villagers agreed to take us to the *guelta* and show us the paintings beside it. We set off up the gorge, a cluster of children following in our wake. The gorge itself was perhaps thirty-five metres deep, scoured out of the sandstone. A few oleanders and the occasional thorn bush flourished where their roots had found their way into crevices in the rocky floor of the gorge.

The *guelta* was three or four hundred metres up the gorge and just below it, on the right-hand side, was a long rock shelter about five metres above the gorge's floor. Here, according to our local guide, were the paintings. The cave did not seem at all familiar, but I climbed up to its entrance, thinking that perhaps I would recognise it when I got inside – as indeed I might have, once.

Nothing I had seen in the Tassili above Djanet had prepared me for this. The cave ran along the side of the gorge for about forty metres. Its height varied between about a metre and a half and three metres, as did its depth. The walls and roof probably contained perhaps a hundred prehistoric paintings, possibly more. Scarcely one was undamaged: almost the entire rock face of the cave had been covered in scribbles, mostly in Arabic and *tifinagh*, new graffiti painting, mostly in black and yellow paint, the colour of road markings, and a general scratching of the rock surface. Paintings had been removed in two places, but it looked as though the rock might have simply been dislodged, rather than cut out. The cave had not just been desecrated – it had been 'trashed'.

I was too shocked and transfixed myself to notice the reaction of my companions immediately. I seem to recall that they were all rather silent. For a couple of days now I had been describing these paintings to them as some of the most beautiful I had seen. And we had all been agreed that if paintings in a remote place such as this had been damaged, then the situation in the Tassili and the Sahara as a whole was probably pretty grim. Bahedi's reaction, I know, was perhaps the most moving. He had seen many of the paintings and engravings in and around Ahaggar, and was well aware of the value and importance of the paintings in archaeological terms. But he had not seen the great sites of Sefar and Jabbaren on the Tassili plateau, and had found it hard to visualise the damage to the Tassili paintings that I had described on my return to Djanet. Now, confronted by this ghastly ruination, he was visibly moved. I sensed a deep anger in him as he prowled rather than walked back and forth in front of the cave's entrance. '*C'est une catastrophe. Vraiment, c'est une véritable catastrophe,*' he said repeatedly to me and to the others, clenching and unclenching his hands as he spoke. Nagim, Moustaffa and Hamed were also clearly upset; Hamdi and Agag sat talking to the villager, but they too, I think, were shocked by what they had seen.

I began to work along the rock face, photographing it in detail, Nagim holding a lens cap against the rock to give me a measure of scale. He spotted them first, I think – a group of figures less than thirty centimetres high, with their heads scraped off. Nearby there were others, just torso and limbs remaining. A cold sensation ran through me and I called Bahedi to come and have a look.

'What do you think of these?' I asked him, pointing to the headless people.

'They haven't got heads.'

'That's right. And do you know what's been happening in Libya?'

'What?'

'Islamic fundamentalists have been coming down into the south and destroying the rock paintings by removing the heads. They think they are pre-Islamic Gods.'

'You're kidding!'

'I don't think so. That's what archaeologists working there have told me. I don't know how widespread it is.'

'Do you think that's what this is?'

'Who knows? But look at them – they've been very carefully scraped off – there's not a trace of the heads left. In Libya, I'm told, there are Tuareg who have been going around touching them up, repainting them! They take offence at their paintings being damaged.'

'I can't imagine Tuareg doing that here,' he said.

'I don't think this is tourists,' I countered. 'Tourists wouldn't remove just the heads; and there's too much Arabic script.' I also couldn't imagine how tourists would get to this place.

'No,' he said, 'I think this is probably the children in the village. It's close to the *guelta*, and they probably come up here to play.'

'Then who the hell is telling the kids to cut the heads off? Isn't there a headman or a Chef du Poste for the Park? Someone who can explain to the children and the rest of the villagers what these paint-ings are?'

'The Chef du Poste is away. That's what they said over in the main village.'

'Then why not leave a message with his friend here, saying that he's going to be put in prison? That'll give him something to con-centrate his mind!' I was furious because of the paintings, but also because of all the other things being done in this country in the name of Islamic fundamentalism; I was also remembering the village headman who had given me so much trouble here thirty-odd years ago.

While I struggled with my anger, Bahedi strolled across to where the villager sat with Hamdi and Agag. As he returned, I was surprised to see that he was chuckling to himself, and there was a mischievous look on his face. I could also see that he was keen to leave. So were we all. It was as if each extra minute we stayed would demand a penance.

11

Ahellakane
discovering the homes of Neolithic man

O UR STAY IN Tamdjert was even shorter than my last visit there, and ended on a similarly disagreeable note. By midday we were back on the plateau, retracing our steps to Tin Haberti. As we dropped off the high plateau on to the shelf just before the ramp, we made a halt for lunch. At my suggestion we settled in the shade of a pile of massive boulders, each one the size of a double-decker bus. It was here, under these same rocks, that I had spent my first night after my 'banishment' from Tamdjert all those years ago. Not that I had recognised it when we drove past the previous evening, but now it was all coming back to me. To make a more comfortable hollow to sleep in, I had dug into the sand that had drifted into the more pro-tected corners, and in the sand I had found several almost completely intact pots, and realised that this shelter had been well-used by Neolithic man thousands of years before. As Moustaffa prepared lunch, the rest of us wandered around to see what else remained. Shards of broken pottery are of little interest to most Tuareg, and the focus of attention quickly reverted to the subject of Ahellakane.

It seemed that none of us had ever been into Ahellakane, though I thought Hamdi was a little equivocal on the subject. I suspected he *had* been there, but didn't want to be regarded as an expert guide, especially as he was going to help us find Kel Tourha who knew the area. I knew Bahedi had been wanting to explore the region for ages, as I had. Nagim, whom I was coming to like more and more as we spent time together, was perhaps more excited than any of us at the prospect of discovering 'unknown places'. For Moustaffa, who hardly ever left Tamanrasset, all was new and very exciting.

Ahellakane would be the ultimate test of our thesis regarding the spread of rock art vandalism, such as it was: we needed to explore the most remote parts of Ahaggar and the Tassili, and Ahellakane was virtually 'unknown'. Apart from an occasional passing Tuareg, Bahedi had found no one in Tamanrasset who was able to enlighten him about the region. For us all, Ahellakane was 'unexplored' territory. If there were any unknown and untouched prehistoric rock paintings left to be found, it was in Ahellakane and in the two adjacent massifs of Atafaitafa and Adrar Hagarhene that we were most likely to find them. And we liked the names: 'Ahellakane' and 'Atafaitafa' had a certain musical ring to them. If Mokhtar could make a song out of 'Garamantes', what might he not do with 'Atafaitafa'?

But how were we going to get to Ahellakane? As far as the map and conventional route-planning went, the answer was simply to retrace our route down off the plateau, past Tin Haberti and then around the southern margins of the Tihodaine sand sea until we picked up the Djanet–Amguid *piste*, a distance of nearly a hundred kilometres. After about two hundred and forty kilometres that *piste* – or what over the years had become hundreds of tracks spread across many kilometres of gravel plain – would take us past Ahellakane's south-facing scarp. Altogether, it was a fairly straightforward drive of about seven hours.

That was the obvious way; but even before Tamdjert we had been talking about the possibility of finding a passage between the sand sea of Tihodaine and the scarp of which Tin Haberti was the highest and most prominent section in this part of the Tassili. This might cut fifty or sixty kilometres off our journey, but its real attraction was that it would take us into what could only be described, even in Saharan terms, as a 'secret valley'. The land between Tihodaine and the scarp was cloud-cuckoo-land, the Land of Dreams. It was hidden, completely cut off from the outside world by the sand sea on one side and a six-hundred-metre vertical wall of rock on the other. Its floor was the ancient bed of what had once been the inland lake of Tihodaine. In Palaeolithic times elephants, other wild animals and early Stone Age man had lived by its shores, followed by Neolithic man, whose vandalised art we had just seen.

Our maps were old, and it wasn't clear from them whether there was a passage between the sand dunes and the scarp. Even Hamdi, the only one of us who had a good knowledge of the area, was uncertain. He had never been in behind Tihodaine, but in chatting to some of the villagers at Tamdjert he had heard that 'there might be a way through'. That was quite enough for Nagim: the merest whiff of adventure, and he was hot in pursuit. I had been intrigued by what lay behind Tihodaine since my first acquaintance with the Sahara, and Bahedi too had fallen in love with this strange region.

We were all so excited at the prospect of what we might find hidden away between Tihodaine and the scarp that not only did the broken pottery we turned up fail to hold our attention, but Moustaffa's excellent lunch of tuna fish, fresh lettuce salad and dried bread was rather unceremoniously disposed of. Instead of following our previous day's route and leaving Tin Haberti to one side, we now headed straight towards it. As we did so, we could see that the dunes ran right up onto the rocky scree slope at the base of the scarp; if we were to get in between Tihodaine and the scarp, we had either to pick our way along this steep and rocky slope, or take our chances on the sand. Nagim chose the slope, and we inched our way forward at no more than walking pace over the loose rock beneath Tin Haberti's huge, craggy bluff. Nagim, Bahedi and I in the front vehicle were craning our necks to see what lay around the long corner. It took us about half an hour of crawling along the scree slope before we finally rounded Tin Haberti and could see what lay in store. To our right, extending as far as we could see, was the long scarp of the Tassili, its black sandstones rising almost vertically from the light yellow floor into a pale blue sky. To our left, running parallel to the scarp face, was the north-eastern side of Tihodaine, with its yellow dunes up to a hundred metres high. Between the two was what we had hoped for: a corridor, a valley, a divide, not much more than a kilometre across at its widest point and mostly only a few hundred metres, between the dunes and the scarp. Its floor, the ancient bed of Lake Tihodaine, was flat gravel, like Amadror. It was as if something held the dunes and the rock face apart, as like is repelled by like in a magnetic field.

In the glare of the afternoon sun I at first had difficulty picking up the outline of the dunes, but as I stared at them I began to see that they were covered with thin black lines, like a cluster of old-fashioned telegraph wires – except that there were no telegraph poles. The lines ran parallel to the gravel floor from the top of the dune slope to the bottom, for as far as I could see.

'What are those?' I asked, pointing them out to Nagim and Bahedi.

'Tracks,' replied Nagim, staring at them enviously.

'But who on earth is driving vehicles through here, and up on the dunes?'

'Bandits, smugglers,' replied Bahedi, resignedly, as if to say 'who else (apart from us) would attempt to cut through here?'

'However can they drive up there?' I asked Nagim. My respect for his knowledge in such matters was already profound. All I could think of was the circus 'Wall of Death' riders I had watched in a state of abject fear and amazement as a child.

'They drive "Stations". They can travel very fast over dunes.'

'Like Louar's?' I asked tentatively, remembering what Nagim had said about the time he once sat in it with him.

'The same,' he said. 'Exactly the same.'

I suspect Nagim's thoughts and my own were similar at that moment: what might he, the Great Hunter, not do with a 'Station'? There certainly wouldn't be so many *mouflon* or gazelles grazing the desert.

The tracks on the dunes were the answer to a question I had been pondering ever since we passed that convoy on the road out of Tamanrasset. It was simply this: if you were a bandit such as Louar or a smuggler running cigarettes, arms, or whatever else from the countries to the south of Algeria into northern Algeria, how would you get there? More specifically, how would you get past, through or over the great wall of the Tassili scarp which presents an almost impenetrable barrier to motor transport across much of southern Algeria?

We had stopped the vehicles and I had pulled out a map and was looking at it with Bahedi. There were not many possible answers to my question. To the east there was absolutely no way of driving across this barrier except by the *piste* from Djanet to Illizi, an obvious route that was almost certainly well guarded by the military and the *gendarmerie*. To the west of us only the two gorges of Arak and Amguid allowed motor passage, both also well-guarded and hence risky. That left only two solutions: one was to keep far to the west of Tamanrasset, roughly in line with the ranges of Tin Ghergoh, Tin Missao and Ahnet; the other was to find another passage through the

Tassili. We pored over the maps with the second of these options in mind. The more we studied them, the more it appeared that the only possible way through the Tassili was to follow this corridor we had found between Tihodaine and the scarp, to a point where the corridor seemed to become submerged in sand. At that point it looked as if one might be able to reach a pass cutting through into a series of valleys that threaded between the massifs of Atafaitafa and Adrar Hagarhene to emerge eventually on the northern side of the mountainous barrier. It was a region through which none of us, not even Hamdi, had ever travelled, but the map suggested that it was feasible, and literally hundreds of tracks were pointing us in that direction.

This corridor in which we now found ourselves was without doubt one of the most scenic places in the Sahara: to our right the great scarp of the Tassili; to our left the dunes of Tihodaine. Its historical significance could but add to its sublimity: shards of pottery and stone artefacts lay scattered almost everywhere we looked on the narrow gravel plain. When we weren't looking for these indications of ancient occupation, Nagim and Hamed drove like teenagers let loose on an empty Grand Prix circuit; fortunately, perhaps, the top speed of a laden, diesel-powered Toyota Land Cruiser is not much over a hundred kilometres an hour.

Here and there along the corridor, close to the base of the scarp, rivulets of scrubby, dried-up pasture waited for the regenerating rainwater that occasionally ran off the scarp. Hamdi had already told me that nomads sometimes came here after good rains, but that traditionally the grazing rights had always been a matter of dispute because the line between the scarp and the sands of Tihodaine marked the border between the Kel In Tunin Tuareg, whom we had just visited at Tamdjert, and Hamdi's own Kel Tourha.

We stopped a couple of times, first because the engines were overheating, then for afternoon prayers. The larger the group, I had noticed, the more assiduous was the observance of such rituals. While the engines cooled we walked around for almost half an hour, looking for stone-age tools and implements. Hamdi, a true man of the desert, had a particularly good eye for things shaped by man rather than nature, but Moustaffa was the most enthusiastic about our finds, and perhaps the most knowledgeable – probably, I suspected, because he was well aware of their value on the tourist market in Tamanrasset! When the time came for afternoon prayers we had driven some forty kilometres along the corridor and were nearing what I suspected was literally the end of the road. The distance between the dunes and the scarp had narrowed to about two or three hundred metres, and ahead of us the corridor looked to be completely blocked by sand. Crispy white patches of salt deposits underfoot suggested that this sand was also a barrier to whatever water occasionally flowed along the corridor.

The corridor was indeed blocked, by millions, perhaps billions of tons of sand, rising to almost a hundred metres in front of us. Tihodaine had finally overcome the forces holding it back for the past fifty kilometres, and was now attacking the scarp with a vengeance. Fancy suggested it must sense that the scarp was lower and more vulnerable here, but more likely the topography had produced a funnel-effect in combination with the wind, drawing the sand in towards the scarp. From whatever cause, the sand was piled high against the black rock face.

Tracks led directly up and over the huge bank of sand. However unpromising it looked, this did seem to be where the bandits found their passage through the Tassili. We stopped at the bottom to assess the daunting proposition. I was the only prophet of doom: I could not see our two Land Cruisers getting anywhere near the top. Even if they did, what lay beyond? Ten, fifteen kilometres of great wallowing sand sea in which the vehicles would almost certainly become trapped, ultimately buried. Both Hamed and Nagim, the two drivers, were raring to go. Even Bahedi, normally so circumspect, seemed oblivious to any danger.

Nagim wanted Hamed to go first, probably so that he could see how the sand lay. I sat in the front passenger seat beside him, watching as Hamed attacked the huge dune. Roaring in at full speed he took the first couple of hundred metres up the slope without difficulty, getting more than half-way up before losing momentum and becoming bogged down in soft sand. Moustaffa, Hamdi and Agag worked with shovels and sand ladders to free the vehicle; once free, Hamed swung first to the left and then to the right, probing for hard sand; but each time he foundered again and had to be dug out. Nagim had seen enough to make him try a route about two hundred metres nearer the scarp face, where he thought the sand might be more compacted. I got out and began the long, arduous walk up the dune face while Nagim launched his vehicle. Briefly I thought he would make it, but just as it seemed that he had broken the back of the slope, he hit soft sand and lurched to a halt. Three times he tried, taking a slightly more diagonal route up the dune face each time. By now I had reached the crest, and Bahedi had gone to join Hamed and the others where they were stuck half-way. Finally, on the fourth attempt, Nagim made it. He powered his way up the far side of the slope and came towards me, accelerating slightly as he crested the dune.

I thought he would stop beside me to survey the lie of the land. Ahead of us the dune swept down for about four hundred metres into a deep trough, surrounded on all sides by huge walls of sand some fifty-odd metres in height, and beyond them, as far as the eye could see, more huge, rolling dunes and equally deep troughs in which vehicles like ours would be simply swallowed up and trapped. But instead of stopping, Nagim continued to accelerate past me. I thought he had gone mad, that he was going to follow the bandit tracks leading down into the huge bowl of sand. Once there, he would have no chance of getting out. I tried to yell, but he was fifty metres beyond me and beginning to drop out of sight. He would anyway never have heard me over the wind and the noise of the engine. Then, right on the lip of the huge trough, he stopped. I walked towards him, trying not to look flustered by his daredevil brinkmanship.

He had got out of the Toyota, and was gazing into the trough.

'What do you think?' I asked, as calmly as I could.

'I think we had better go around.'

'Yes,' I said. 'Getting stuck down there could be a bit tricky.'

Nagim clambered into the vehicle, turned it around, and headed back down the long slope. I breathed a sigh of relief, and abandoned my visions of the *gendarmes* from Ideles setting off in search of us. I could imagine only too well what they would have had to say about a bunch of Tuareg who had managed to 'drown' a Land Cruiser in a sand sea! 'I'll walk,' I said as he passed me, and set off to lend the others a hand. By now they were unveiled, stripped to their under-shirts, and exhausted. Hamed's vehicle had got itself heavily bogged down in a soft patch of sand about half-way down the slope. Before leaving the crest I paused to admire the bandit tracks carved across the huge sweeps of sand that had defeated us. It was those tracks, I suspected, and his envy of their Stations' superior performance in sand which had driven Nagim to the summit in the first place and then lured him so very close to the edge of disaster.

As I turned to leave the crest, I noticed a stone arrowhead lying on the sand by my feet. Picking it up, I admired its exquisite workmanship. Had it fallen out of a wounded animal as it ran to safety thousands of years ago, I wondered, or had the wind whisked it, like a paper dart, to the very top of the dune?

It was hard to accept that the bandits had got the better of us! We so itched to find out what sort of passage was hidden by the dunes! Bahedi, Nagim and I even discussed the possibility of trying to cross the neck of sand by foot – it was only about ten or fifteen kilometres wide – while the two Toyotas drove the hundred and fifty or so kilometres around the shores of Tihodaine to meet us on the other side. But we decided it was foolhardy. In any case, our objective was to get to Ahellakane. So, disappointed at having come so close to achieving our 'short cut', and exhausted from almost two hours of trudging and digging in sand, we retraced our tracks along the corridor to Tin Haberti, and made camp for that night on a tongue of low dunes on the eastern side of Tihodaine.

We all slept well. Certainly we were tired from our exertions in the sand, but it's a fact that there is something very restful and calming about sleeping under the stars on dunes. My ruptured sleeping bag had been replaced with blankets and one of Bahedi's camping mattresses. This was more comfortable than a sleeping bag, especially since it was not as cold here as on the Tassili or in the Tefedest. That night as I lay on the dune breathing the cool night air I made my own journeys through the stars, which on this moonless night were displaying themselves in all their glory. Waking before dawn, I lay in the warmth of my blankets and watched the first light and then the rim of the sun break the eastern horizon. The desert was utterly quiet and pure in that first short hour of the day. No one stirred as each of the six others lying scattered over the dune enjoyed the last few moments of sleep.

We left early, our breakfast no more than a cup of coffee to wash down a few mouthfuls of *tagella*, dipped in the sickly-sweet apricot jam that must rival tinned sardines as colonialism's most profound legacy to Saharan nutrition. We were in good humour: I think that after the disappointment of Tamdjert and the failure of our short cut, we all cherished an unfounded hope that today would turn out better. Early morning is always the best time of the day to cross the desert. The light is good, the heat of the day has not built up, and sand is more compact and easier to drive on (as the day wears on, the air between the sand grains heats up and expands, making the sand more unstable and 'softer').

By the time the sun was beginning to make itself felt we had retraced our route around the eastern and southern edges of Tihodaine, and were making good progress up the west side of the sand sea towards the point we might have reached the previous evening if our passage behind Tihodaine had not been blocked. As we turned to head up the western side of Tihodaine we passed an outcrop of three rocky hills, each about eight hundred metres long and rising perhaps a hundred metres above the gravel plain. They were less than two kilometres from the edge of the sand sea, and in Palaeolithic times were probably islands in the lake, or higher ground standing above the marshes around its shoreline. The first and largest of the three was covered by at least twenty huge circular stone prehistoric burial tombs, and had clearly been a place of great sacred significance.

For the rest of the morning we continued in a west-north-westerly direction, once again driving parallel and close to the Tassili scarp. Hamdi's main job now was to find his Kel Tourha kinsmen living in this region who, he had told us, could guide us into Ahellakane. Without him it would have been like looking for a needle in a haystack, for the encampment, such as it was, consisted of a cluster of makeshift shelters constructed of tree branches and whatever they had in the way of skins and thatch to serve as awnings, hidden in a cirque or corrie about fifteen kilometres across shaped by a deep bay in the scarp. The basin clearly took a lot of run-off from the scarp, and perhaps even from the plateau behind it, for although there had clearly not been much rain for a while, the whole area was well covered with acacias and other thorn trees. There was also enough pasture, though it looked pretty shrivelled and dry, to graze a reasonable goat herd for most of the year round. And there was plenty of fresh water. Hidden deep in the cirque, with nothing obvious to mark it, was a well which produced good, clear water from a depth of between twenty and twenty-five metres. I don't think I have ever come across a more isolated camp in Ahaggar, nor one that looked so poor. There were no signs of either camels or tents. We refilled our cans at the well, taking turns with the goatskin bucket on a pulley which raised about five litres of water at a time, while Hamdi proceeded on foot and alone to the camp. He returned a short while later accompanied by a man about ten years his junior whom he introduced to us as Erza.

I wondered what Erza made of it all. Suddenly two vehicles and seven people, five of them strangers, had driven into his remote world quite out of the blue to ask him to accompany them on a search for prehistoric paintings! Whatever his private thoughts about this bizarre occurrence, he seemed ready enough for the adventure. I was amazed by the ease with which he slipped from his remote and isolated life as a simple herdsman into the persona of 'special guide', paid at official Tamanrasset rates.

We were now eight, sitting on blankets spread out under the acacia. Hamed had made tea, which we drank as Moustaffa devoted himself to producing one of his wonderful lunches – his 'magic' food chest seemed to contain an endless supply of fresh salad. Erza had thrown his personal bedding into the back of one of the Toyotas and was sitting next to Hamdi, already the centre of conversation with questions being politely fired at him from all sides. Hamdi and Agag, Kel Tourha themselves, wanted to catch up on family and 'tribal' news, while Bahedi and Nagim were trying to find out about rock art sites and access to them. It was an extraordinary scene. A stranger stumbling into our midst might well have thought that we were interrogating a newly-captured prisoner.

Erza was typical of almost every nomadic Tuareg I have ever met in that he could give us details of every rock, every plant and every nook and cranny within a two-day ride, and probably much further beyond as well. But when it came to rock art, it was another matter altogether. Yes, he told us, he had seen quite a few paintings around and about, but he wasn't very interested in them. He could take us to a few caves in which there were paintings and 'stones', and if he thought about it for a little longer, he would probably remember quite a few more. If someone had asked him to look out for such things, he told us, then he would have done so. But no one had ever asked him. The gist of it was that, like so many Tuareg, he simply wasn't 'into primitive art'.

After lunch, Erza readily climbed into the back seat of the other vehicle, between Hamdi and Agag. As 'cousins' living at opposite ends of the Tourha mountains they had a lot to catch up on: two hundred and fifty kilometres is quite a way to travel on foot or camel.

Erza had whetted our appetites. He seemed to know of several caves with paintings, but they were all a couple of days' walk away. However, he also claimed to know a spot about twenty-five kilo-metres back along the scarp where vehicles had once driven up it. Casting my mind back along the length of scarp past which we had just driven, I had grave doubts: surely it would have been suicidal to try to get a vehicle up it anywhere. Like me, Bahedi was pretty scep-tical, and he and I set about discussing the feasibility of the walk involved. But Hamdi, who had been quizzing Erza narrowly, reck-oned he might be on to something. When we got to the point on the scarp Erza had been talking about, I could see no sign of a track. The scarp was broken into two levels here, rather like the entrance to Tamdjert, and probably there were passages through the higher scarp. Yet I could see no conceivable way of getting a vehicle up to the first level. Presumably the vehicle Erza had once seen here had belonged to the military, or perhaps a geological survey.

Nagim and Hamed first walked up the scarp face to assess the practicalities. When they returned, Nagim said he thought it might be possible if the rest of us cleared some of the bigger boulders out of the way. No one but Nagim, I thought, would have been crazy enough to try it, and I was surprised that Bahedi was willing to let him have a go. The consequences, if the vehicle slipped and rolled, would have been calamitous. Once again, I felt a pang of sympathy for the unsuspecting *gendarmes* at Ideles! Bahedi and I were both glad to be delegated to moving boulders, admitting to each other a fear of heights and propensity to vertigo. Moustaffa too seemed happy enough to move boulders. Hamdi, Agag and Erza, in true nomad spirit, remained slightly aloof from the whole operation, doubtless particularly bewildered by the fuss we 'townies' (Bahedi, Moustaffa and I) were making. They moved a few stones in an inconsequential sort of way, but for them a Toyota or a Land Rover was, in terms of its usefulness, merely a latter-day version of a camel or a donkey – or perhaps a souped-up cross between the two, with the speed of a gazelle.

Whether Nagim or Toyota should take the credit is debatable, but they made it, more easily than I had anticipated, with Nagim leading and Hamed following close behind.

The shelf was much more expansive than I had imagined, running for many kilometres in both directions, and the upper scarp was broken in many places by small passes and wider valley entrances. Erza was in his element, for this was a land he knew as few others did. He guided us for almost an hour in twists and turns through rocky defiles, past patches of sand blown up from the plain below, sometimes almost doubling back on ourselves. We finally came to a halt in a short valley cluttered with boulders and fine sand which made progress difficult. At the valley's head, two boulder-strewn gorges descended from yet a third tier of plateau above. A few stunted thorn trees and patches of dried-up pasture in the valley floor indicated that occasional rain was channelled down the gorges.

From here, Erza explained, we would have to walk for about an hour up the left-hand gorge on to the high plateau, and then for several kilometres through a maze of little valleys feeding into the gorge. None of us knew more of where Erza was taking us than that it was to some caves where there were paintings. Given his complete lack of interest in such things, there was no way of knowing whether we were about to see the Neolithic equivalent of the *Mona Lisa*, or mere amateurish daubings.

When we got there, we found it was nearer to the *Mona Lisa*. Erza had taken us into another world, to the top of the Tassili, nearly a thousand metres above his camp, somewhere between Ahellakane, Atafaitafa and the Adrar Hagarhene. It was more like a jungle of broken-up lesser mountain tops than a plateau, further dissected by a chaotic network of small, heavily weathered valleys – some sandy, some bare rock – bounded by low and often jagged cliffs that had provided those prehistoric hunters and herdsmen who once inhabited this remarkable land with an almost limitless choice of rock shelters and caves.

The first shelter to which Erza took us was truly breathtaking. The paintings were fabulous, depicting a range of both hunting and Bovidian period scenes, and also 'round-heads', suggesting a long period of either permanent or intermittent settlement. What was truly magical, however, was that the shelter seemed completely untouched by modern man, even passing nomads. Stone implements that had been used by Neolithic man were still lying in place on the ground and on ledges in the shelter. On one such stone ledge, half a dozen pestles and grinding stones and a handful of smaller stones of no obvious usage had been set out as neatly as if on a pantry shelf. They might possibly have been put there comparatively recently by passing nomads, but I doubted it: Tuareg have a tendency to take such stones and re-use them for the same age-old purposes in their own camps. Like other sites I recalled from thirty years ago, it looked as if the shelter's last occupants had simply walked away one day, never to return.

As I sat in the entrance, trying to take in the magnificence, and revelling in the sheer privilege of being able to see a shelter in this state, I realised that Henri Lhote, Yolande Tschudi and many others must have experienced similar feelings when they first came across such fantastic treasures from so long ago. It would have been nice to stay there for a few days, mooching around on my own, absorbing the atmosphere and mentally reconstructing the lives that had been lived here so many thousands of years ago. *This* was what I had hoped to find. I needed to know that at least part of the Tassili – the world's greatest art gallery – had not yet been despoiled. Deliberately I refrained from thinking about the obvious questions – For how long? And what can be done to safeguard it? I wanted to immerse myself and revel in a sight few have experienced, the like of which I realised I might never see again.

I was brought back to the present by fits of laughter from Nagim and Bahedi, who were sitting on a rock outcrop on the far side of the shelter.

'What's so funny?' I asked.

'Any minute now we are going to come across the Chef du Poste from Tamdjert,' said Nagim. He couldn't stop laughing.

I still didn't see the joke.

'You remember when we were walking back down the gorge at Tamdjert yesterday, after seeing all the ruined paintings? Well, when Bahedi was chatting to the man from the village, he told him that we were going back to Tamanrasset to report the Chef du Poste for allowing all the damage, and that he would be taken and sent to prison!'

Now I knew why Bahedi had had such a mischievous grin on his face.

'He'll never dare go back to Tamdjert,' said Bahedi, who was also still beside himself with laughter. 'Just imagine him spending the rest of his life roaming up here with his goats like a nomad!'

It *was* funny. If Bahedi's leg-pull gave the wretched man a few sleepless nights, it was no more than he deserved.

Once Erza had seen our excitement and understood the sort of caves and paintings we were looking for, he was able to take us to many others. For two days we trekked around this most amazing of places, returning to sleep on the ground by the vehicles at night. It was like being on another planet to know that, apart from the occasional nomad like Erza, we were probably the first people for countless centuries to walk through this chaotic landscape with its magnificent views across the various Tassili massifs to the north, east and west, and towards Ahaggar and the mountains of Tourha far to the south. Like children with too many presents, after a while we became blasé.

As we discovered one cave after another, the novelty almost began to wear off, and we tended to be dismissive when a cave or shelter did not match up to expectations. Nagim, the Great Hunter of only two days before, now became the Great Archaeologist. He had heard of the Tassili rock paintings, of course, but I do not think that he had seen any before this journey. On the way here I had told him what I could of their 'discovery', the dating of them and the various styles and so on, but he was genuinely overwhelmed by what we were now seeing, and scampered like a man possessed from one valley or outcrop to another 'discovering' new paintings. In one of 'his' shelters I photographed him standing against the rock face so that his head was positioned between a group of exquisitely-painted young girls and an elaborate hunting scene.

'There you are,' I said. 'The true hunter: women on one side, wild animals on the other!'

'Ah, "the new Henri Lhote",' he retorted, laughing and holding his arms outstretched.

'No, it should be "the new Jebrine",' said Bahedi, and explained to him that it was Jebrine, Lhote's Tuareg guide, who had 'discovered' most of the paintings. Laughing at Nagim's antics, Bahedi then asked me if I knew that Jebrine had only died quite recently.

'Is that so? I know he was well over sixty when he worked with Lhote – he was said to have been born around 1890 or 1892. He must have been getting on for a hundred, then?'

'I think he probably was,' said Bahedi. 'You know that he was telling people that Lhote didn't pay him properly?'

'That's no surprise,' I said. 'In his book, Lhote described the Tuareg as living like wolves!'

During his lifetime, all Tuareg had regarded Jebrine as knowing the Tassili better than anyone. Now that he was dead, it was good to hear him being discussed with such high regard and respect by his own people. Without doubt, it is Jebrine's name rather than Lhote's that will be remembered longest and most affectionately by the people of Ahaggar and the Tassili.

We would have been happy to stay with Erza for many more days, but my time was limited and we still had plans to explore the Tassili-ta-n Tin Ghergoh, some eight hundred kilometres away on the far side of Ahaggar. And so, sad to leave but elated by what we had seen, we retraced our way back down the scarp to Erza's camp, where we left him, happy with a handsome bonus for being such an excellent guide and travelling companion, and all our surplus food supplies.

12

Stinking nightshade in the devil's kitchen garden

WE LEFT ERZA at his camp at about three in the afternoon. Both Hamdi and Agag wanted to shop in Tamanrasset before returning to their camps (probably to buy provisions with the money they had earned with us as guides), so we decided to take the shortest and quickest possible route. This meant travelling more or less in a straight line in a south-south-westerly direction, which would take us across the north-western corner of Amadror, through the Tourha mountains and across the great Irharhar valley to the northern end of Tefedest, down the eastern side of Tefedest to the *Oued* Mertoutek (where we thought we would drop in on Mokhtar), and then directly to Tamanrasset. The distance was around eight hundred kilometres, about fifteen hours of driving.

By late afternoon we had covered something over a hundred kilometres; we were midway down the western edge of Amadror and, by my calculations, only about fifteen kilometres to the west of Tisemt. Although the land here is as flat as the rest of Amadror, its surface is quite different, a black-and-white patchwork of salt deposits and lava. The lava looks as though a few million medium-sized lumps of coal fallen from a flotilla of lorries have been raked out to make a level surface. Had the patches been perfect squares, we might have been travelling over a giant chess-board. I had no idea Nature could be so kitsch.

The spot where we chose to camp that night was even more surreal. The chess-board was bisected by a swathe of deep bottle-green in the form of a wide but very shallow *oued* whose bed was

197

filled by the most obnoxious-looking plants. None was much more than about sixty centimetres tall, and the larger specimens were about a hundred and fifty centimetres across. Quite apart from their virulent colour and foetid smell, the very shape of the plants was offputting, their fleshy, upward-pointing leaves giving them a spiky, grasping appearance. Amid the green foliage lurked scant numbers of tiny purple flowers. They too were uninviting, as was the *oued* itself. Its bed, far from being full of clean sand and gravel, was clogged with dirty-white, caked crusts of salt, lumps of coal-black lava and smoother, pure white slabs of a plastic-looking calcareous material.

'There you are,' said Bahedi. '*Efelehleh.*'

'I don't believe it,' I said. 'All this?'

'As far as the eye can see. Probably enough to poison half the world.'

This was the plant the Tuareg had used to poison the survivors of the Flatters massacre. It grows in only a few remote parts of Ahaggar, and Bahedi knew that I had very much wanted to find it. Here it was, in almost rampant profusion. Mention it to Tuareg and they will probably start to chuckle, as they do whenever anything connected with this episode of their history is referred to.

Since first reading about what befell the Flatters expedition I had acquired an almost obsessive interest in this plant. Its botanical name is *Hyoscyamus muticus* subspecies *falezlez*, a member of the potato family, the Solonaceae, which also includes the deadly nightshade. The henbane or *la jusquiame* of Britain and France is *H. niger*, named in fact from the colour of the seeds, but wholly appropriately in view of its long association with witchcraft and death; another common name is corpse flower. In his French–Tamahak dictionary, Foucauld referred to it as '*la jusquiame de l'Ahaggar*'.

I examined it more closely, walking from one specimen to another, and as I did so became aware of a curious rustling noise, which I thought must be made by some sort of cricket. Then I noticed that almost every plant was shrouded in spiders' webs. The sound must be made by spiders, scuttling about in the dry sandy depths of the plants. It was quite a shock, for I suddenly remembered an obscure report I had once come across, on the use of henbane in India, which noted that people who had been poisoned by it (and, presumably, survived) recounted hallucinations of being chased by knee-high spiders!

'So here it is: the present the Tuareg gave the survivors of the Flatters massacre,' said Bahedi.

'Do you think this is the *oued* where they found the *efelehleh*?'

'It could be. It's not so far from Amguid.'

It was extraordinary to think that this very patch of obscene-looking vegetation might have played a significant part in the history of North Africa. And if the *efelehleh* used on that occasion hadn't come from here, it was probably from somewhere close by.

'According to the report,' I said, 'the Tuareg mixed it with crushed dates and offered it to the survivors as they trekked back to Amguid. But only the French soldiers ate it; the Chaambi knew that such generosity from Tuareg was bound to be a trick.'

'Quite right,' laughed Bahedi. 'And it killed them?'

'It seems to have been rather worse than that,' I replied. 'From what I can make out, death was a rather grisly and long-drawn-out process in which the victims were first driven demented and actually tried to kill one another.'

'Why did they do that?'

'The *efelehleh* drove them mad. There are a lot of pretty potent drugs in that plant. Apart from the hallucinatory elements, it makes the body, and especially the skin, feel hot and swollen. According to the survivors' reports, some of the French soldiers just rushed off into the desert, stripping off their clothes and shooting at one another. I think the report even said something about self-mutilation with knives.'

There was still half an hour of daylight left as Bahedi and I walked back from the *oued* to where Moustaffa and Hamed had set up camp and were preparing our evening meal. Nagim, Hamdi and Agag were on the point of driving off again in one of the vehicles.

'Where are they going?' I asked.

'Nagim saw a large herd of gazelles in the distance as we arrived, and you know what he's like. One for the pot, perhaps.'

'Do gazelles eat *efelehleh*?'

'It's excellent grazing. Didn't you see how the tips of the plants over there had been nibbled?'

'What about the poison, though?'

'It doesn't affect animals. You just have to make sure you don't eat the stomach of an animal that has been grazing on it.'

'But you can't always tell what a wild animal might have been eating!'

'That's why you sometimes hear of Tuareg being poisoned by it, and occasionally even dying.'

Hamed and Moustaffa came to join us on the carpets by the fire, and began to make tea as we waited for Nagim and the others to return.

'They must have been crazy thinking they could build a railway across the Sahara,' said Bahedi, evidently still thinking about Flatters.

'I think they were,' I agreed. 'But that was the time when the colonial powers thought they could do just about anything, especially in Africa. It wasn't only the French. The English had some pretty crazy schemes too.'

Moustaffa, who usually spent more time listening than talking, said: 'But how did they think they could supply the locomotive with water, coal or wood?'

'That's what people asked the Minister,' I answered.

'And what did he say?'

'He ignored the questions.'

'How typical of a politician,' said Bahedi. 'But didn't the people at Laghouat, or even the Chaamba, warn them of what might happen?'

'That,' I said, 'was probably the funniest thing about the whole crazy plan. Do you know the story of the Tidjani and the *mokhadem* – the holy man?'

'No! What did they have to do with it?'

'Well, as you know, the expedition set off from Laghouat, and Laghouat is close to the headquarters of the Tidjani sect. A few years before, in the 1870s, the head of the sect, Si Ahmed, who was fabulously wealthy, had married a young French girl – Aurélie Picard – and she had set up her home in Laghouat. Colonel Flatters was pretty gung-ho about the expedition, unlike the other French involved. The Chaamba, who knew only too well that the apparent friendliness of the Tuareg was a lot of nonsense, were openly fearful. Aurélie decided to boost French courage by holding a grand dinner, awash with the finest champagne, and at the dinner she tried to rally their spirits and their courage, telling them it was imperative that they penetrate the legendary land of the Tuareg, otherwise it would remain forever barred to France.'

'Why?' interjected Bahedi.

'Because the Turks had their eye on it.'

'What about the Chaamba, though?'

'That's where the holy man came in. To overcome the fears of the Chaamba and the other Moslem auxiliaries, Aurélie arranged for a *mokhadem* of the Tidjani order to be attached to the expedition. The *mokhadem*, she said, would ensure the safety of the Moslem members of the expedition, and also that of the infidels. The influence of the Tidjanis extended over the whole of the Sahara, as far as the river Niger, and not even the Tuareg, said Aurélie, would dare molest a Tidjani holy man.'

'That sounds like the right recipe for courage,' said Bahedi. 'Alcohol for one and religion for the other.'

'Absolutely!' I could only laugh at his neat summing-up.

'And how did the *mokhadem* fare among the Tuareg?'

'Not very well,' I said. 'In fact, he came off worst of all. After the business with the *efelehleh*, the survivors had to pass through the Amguid gorge, at the western end of Ahellakane, which was the only source of water. The Tuareg had been keeping just out of range, on their flanks, and just before they got to the gorge offered to sell the party some sheep, but demanded that responsible men be sent to negotiate the deal. Thinking that the Tuareg, who were lined up on the cliffs above the gorge, would respect a holy man, the surviving French officer decided to send the *mokhadem* and three Chaamba. As the four men approached the Tuareg they were seized and bound and lined up against the cliff in sight of their companions. The three Chaamba were decapitated in turn. There was a short pause, then the *mokhadem* was split in half from skull to hips with one blow from a *takouba*.'

'Yugh!' exclaimed Moustaffa. 'That wasn't very nice.'

'It's one way of getting the message across,' said Bahedi.

'And it worked,' I said. 'It was the best part of twenty years before the French dared make another push south.'

We sipped tea in silence for a moment, then Moustaffa asked what had happened to those that survived the *efelehleh*.

I remember when I first read the summary report on that expedition: it was like something out of a horror story. I recounted the gist of it to Moustaffa and Bahedi.

'Some died in a battle to get into the gorge at Amguid – the French actually managed to drive the Tuareg out of the gorge. But it was still another eight hundred kilometres back to Ouargla, and they had nothing to eat. They reverted to cannibalism. They were simply killed, one by one, and the survivors ate the flesh. The last Frenchman to be eaten was a Sergeant Pobéguin; thereafter the cook, Private Belkacem, took on the role of professional executioner in addition to preparing the meat. If you wanted to stay alive, you kept your eyes open, and fixed on Belkacem!' I was about to make a joke to Moustaffa about the importance of cooks on desert treks when Nagim's headlights swept up behind us, diverting our thoughts to fresh gazelle meat. In fact he was empty-handed – it had really been too late in the day to chase gazelles – but full of excitement. He had counted fifty gazelles, the largest number he had ever seen in one place. It was, he assured us, the fresh *efelehleh* that had attracted them here.

Bahedi and I put up our one-man tents that night. The pretext was protection against mosquitoes, but I think we both knew it was too cold for them. In truth, it was because I had raised the question of where the spiders we had seen in the *efelehleh* went in the night! Happily we neither felt nor saw any spiders. In the morning, for no particular reason, we made a later start than usual. I suspect it was to do with the depressing nature of the *oued* and its surroundings. In the cold light of morning, there really was a sense of death about it. It was as if the devil had taken it over as his own kitchen garden.

As we were loading up the vehicles and getting ready to leave, I asked Hamdi what the area was called. He didn't know the name of this particular *oued*, but the mountain just to the south-west of it, part of the Tourha range, was called Amzer Oumfat, which struck me as being an appropriately ugly name for an ugly place. When I asked him what it meant, he said 'the thirsty shoulder'. Neither Bahedi, Nagim nor the others could enlighten me as to the significance of the name.

It was good to turn our backs on both the *oued* and the 'thirsty shoulder' and head off into the freshness of the desert. After about eight kilometres we crossed over a col between two low, rocky hills that marked the end of the devil's kitchen garden and brought us into a shallow basin four to six kilometres wide and surrounded by a ring of modest hills. The floor of the basin was pure, clean gravel – no lava, and no salt – and almost as smooth as Amadror, broken just here and there by clusters of slightly bigger stones and small, almost imperceptible rivulet beds which collected into a tiny *oued* and drained out of the basin to the west. The early morning sun directly behind us gave the basin a pristine quality, in marked contrast to the land we had just left.

Nagim, as usual, saw it first: a solitary gazelle. I wondered if it was one of the fifty he had seen the evening before, grazing on the *efeleh-leh*. The poor animal had no chance: it had ventured too far into the centre of the basin, no doubt foraging for fresh pasture where the tiny rivulets came together at the beginning of the *oued*; I reckoned it was a good three kilometres from the encircling hills. Nagim and Hamed, who was following behind, had no need to communicate – they knew the drill too well. Hamed drove slowly to the north of the animal, encouraging it to make a run for the southern side of the basin, where Nagim had already positioned himself, ready to accelerate and to cut if off. The gazelle had covered perhaps a kilometre at speed before it realised it could not make the safety of the southern rim of hills; it turned, instinct heading it back to the north.

It was a male, four or five years old and in the peak of condition. Nagim was most precise: ten kilometres, or maybe eleven, he explained to me, would be enough to exhaust the beast and bring him to his knees.

The gazelle's run to the north proved just as futile, of course, Hamed cutting off this escape and forcing him to look once more to the south. Two, three, four, five runs were made in this way, the gazelle capable each time of bursts of up to forty kilometres an hour. The poor animal was trapped: each run for freedom only brought him closer to the point of exhaustion. Gradually the runs became shorter and his speed less, and the two vehicles were now able to hem him in, forcing him to run in ever-tighter circles. The desert surface was churned into a series of figures-of-eight as each vehicle in turn forced the animal away from his bolt for freedom and into the path of the other. And all the time, almost imperceptibly, we were being drawn ever westwards.

The only chance for the gazelle, it seemed, was for the vehicles to crash, or their suspension to fail. Neither could be ruled out. The rivulets deepened towards the western side of the basin, and on one figure-of-eight manoeuvre a high-speed collision was averted by no more than a metre, amid wild yelps of excitement and a cloud of dust.

Did the gazelle know anything of the ways of these modern-day hunters, I wondered? Certainly he would not give up until his heart gave out. Equally certainly, the hunters would not give up the chase: this was their tradition, their way of life and their excitement. We had no need for the meat, but Tuareg relished it, and could always justify a kill on the 'one for the pot' principle.

As the circles tightened and we closed in, I could see the wild look of desperation and fear in the gazelle's eyes. Whether through ingenuity, animal instinct or chance (I like to think it was the first), somehow the animal had by now drawn us sufficiently far westwards to be close to the *oued*. The drop down into the *oued* at this point was almost a metre, quite enough to smash the suspension. The gazelle bounded down that drop, and for a moment it was a stand-off. Nagim and Hamed had to pause and rethink their tactics. 'Stay there,' I willed the beast. 'Just stay in the *oued* and you are safe.' The *oued* was a sort of no-man's-land, in which vehicles could proceed at little more than walking pace. The gazelle can't have known that, so perhaps it was the sight of the vehicles stationary on either side of the *oued* as he paused to draw breath that gave him the confidence for one last dash across the basin to the safety of the hills. If he had only stayed in the *oued*, he might have stood a chance, but his instinct told him safety lay in the distant hills.

Nagim was on him like a hawk, the front bumper almost touching his tail before he had made a hundred metres. His speed had deserted him and he could manage no more than a trot, but still he did not give up. Each time I thought he must drop, he summoned the energy to put his ears back and make one more leap to the left or to the right, forcing Nagim to put the vehicle into a spin. Each spin carried the chance, if a remote one, of a smashed wheel or suspension.

I do not know how long the chase lasted – at least half an hour, and surely we had covered more than Nagim's ten or eleven kilometres. When the inevitable end came, it was fast. No more than ten metres in front of it, the gazelle turned to face the vehicle, and dropped onto his front knees. It was the most pathetic sight I think I have ever seen involving an animal.

Nagim did not even bother to put on the brake, but left the vehicle rolling forwards as he leapt out, wooden club in hand, and ran towards the gazelle, which raised himself from his knees and managed to stagger another couple of metres. There was no struggle. Death was already very near as the gazelle gasped for air, his eyes, glazed and terrified, seeming to focus on all of us at once. Surely we had been guilty of a crime, while all he had done was walk across the land in the early morning sunlight in search of grazing.

Nagim held all four legs together in one hand, insurance against a final kick from the sharp hooves. With the other hand he ran a razor-sharp dagger across the gazelle's throat. The body jerked a few times and the legs kicked wildly and aimlessly as air gurgled out of the body and the heart, still pumping, sent half a dozen spurts of blood across the unblemished desert surface.

Nagim's expertise with the knife suddenly made me think of the thirty thousand or so people who had been *égorgé* over the last few years in various parts of the country, and I wondered whether the sounds and the spurts of blood were any different. Probably not.

Listening as Nagim and the others justified the kill didn't make me feel any better. Yet hunting has always been part of desert life, and at least the gazelle had now re-established itself in healthy numbers following the depredations of the French, and was providing Tuareg with meat in the time-honoured way. Once the gazelle had been skinned and strung up on the back of the vehicle, we drove on. The pool of blood had already soaked into the desert floor, and the severed head with its once-proud horns was lying on its side. The eyes, wide open, stared sightlessly into the desert sky. The jackals would come in the night and scream that not enough had been left for them; and that would be the end of it.

Conversation flagged after we had all agreed that Nagim was indeed a Great Hunter. We drove on for an hour or more, until we came to a small pool of filthy black salty water. There was nothing about the surrounding landscape and geology to indicate why water, normally many metres below the desert surface, even in *oueds*, should be at ground level at this otherwise unremarkable point. Nor could Hamdi offer any sort of explanation. When I asked him why he had brought us this way, he said he merely wanted to check on it while we were in the region. It was convenient for nomads, of course, since camels could drink directly from it.

A short while later we crossed the Irharhar valley. The Irharhar is the longest *oued* in Ahaggar, probably in the whole Sahara, and its bed is easily a kilometre wide and so shallow as to be almost indistinguishable from the wider valley. In ancient times it is possible that this *oued* may have carried a more constant flow of water, but today it offers scant pasture for the nomads of Tefedest and Tourha between which it runs. By the time we had crossed it, it was nearly midday and the wind had whipped up the dust into a haze. Visibility was reduced to a few kilometres, and as we retraced much of the route I had travelled with Mokhtar not so long ago we could scarcely see the outline of Tefedest to our right.

We found Mokhtar at Dehine. It was very good to see him again, although at first I did not recognise him. He was no longer wearing his customary green *gandoura* and brown shirt, and had veiled himself completely to greet unexpected company. He was thrilled to see both us and the gazelle, and to hear the news of our travels, particularly among the Kel Tourha,with whom he had distant kin ties. The gazelle was devoured by almost everyone in the small settlement during the course of a protracted midday meal. No mention was made of *efelehleh*, but I made sure that the stomach and intestines had been carefully disposed of.

The drive from Mokhtar's to Tamanrasset should have taken no more than six hours, but three punctures on the way were the price we paid for our hunting escapade, and it was approaching midnight by the time we finally arrived back at Bahedi's *gîte*.

13

Tin Ghergoh
land of elephants and mushrooms

AFTER OUR 'DISCOVERIES' in Ahellakane, Bahedi and Nagim especially couldn't wait to get moving again. I think we had all been infected by the sense that we really were exploring unknown places. While that may have been true for Ahellakane, however, the ranges around the south-western margin of Ahaggar, the Tassili-ta-n Ghergoh and the Tassili-ta-n Missao, could not be called 'unexplored'. On the other hand, they were not at all well mapped, and had certainly not been visited by many people in recent years. The reasons for this comparative isolation were quite simple: few if any Tuareg now lived in the area, it had never attracted much tourism, and travel there, difficult in any case because of shifting sand dunes, was now further beset by 'bandits' and smugglers entering Algeria over the nearby Niger and Mali borders.

Nagim arrived at the *gîte* fairly early in the morning following our puncture-ridden drive back from Mertoutek, and joined us for breakfast. Bahedi and I already had the maps out, little use though they were for this part of the Sahara. Nagim wasn't much interested in the maps because, he said, he knew the country between Tamanrasset and the Niger and Mali frontiers pretty well, though he did admit that he had never actually been into the Tassili-ta-n Tin Ghergoh or the Tassili-ta-n Missao ranges.

I was particularly eager to explore the Tin Ghergoh mountains, some three hundred kilometres to the south-west of Tamanrasset. Like Bahedi and Nagim I had never been into them, but they seemed a likely place for extensive prehistoric settlement sites and rock art, and I wanted to see whether the isolation of the region might have safeguarded them from the sort of vandalism we had found in the Tassili-n-Ajjer. And I must admit that after our exploits behind Tihodaine, I was becoming most intrigued by the routes bandits were using to cross in and out of Algeria.

Bahedi was a little less optimistic than Nagim about the trip, knowing that the police would not give us permits to travel in the region unless we were accompanied by a recognised guide – evidently, as far as they were concerned, Nagim did not fall within that category. And scarcely anyone, recognised guide or not, knew those mountains.

'There is only one guide,' said Bahedi pensively, as the five of us – by now Claudia and Moustaffa had joined us – sat over our coffee around the kitchen table.

'Akali?' said Nagim.

Bahedi nodded. 'Precisely.'

Nagim gave a laugh, but didn't say anything.

'What's funny about him?' I asked.

Bahedi also began to chuckle. 'You'll see'

'No. Nothing really,' said Nagim. 'But we tease him.'

'You both know him, then?'

Nagim flicked his wrist. 'Since we were young. We all knew Akali!' Childhood memories inspired him to more laughter.

'Do you know where he is right now?' Bahedi asked.

'Amsel,' Nagim replied.

'Yes, I know,' said Bahedi. 'But is he there *now*?'

'I don't know. I'll go out there this morning. If he's not there, I'll soon find him.' Nagim finished his coffee, had a few words with Bahedi, and set off to find Akali.

'He's a Tegehe-n-Efis,' Bahedi said to me. 'Do you know them?'

'Only that they were traditionally vassel Kel Ulli Tuareg whose lands extended far to the south and south-west of Tamanrasset,' I answered. 'But I never stayed in their camps.'

'Akali was once a famous guide, the best in this region,' said Bahedi. 'But when we were young, he was a bit of a tyrant.'

Nagim returned at the end of the afternoon. He had found Akali at his home, and Akali had agreed to come with us. But there was a huddled conversation between Bahedi and Nagim, obviously none of my business, which left me with the impression that not every-thing had been straightforward. Perhaps he was demanding an outra-geous fee reflecting an inflated estimation of his own worth in what was clearly a seller's market. But Bahedi assured me that there was no such problem, and we were to stop at Amsel and pick him up on our way out to the south-west.

'It's just that he's a bit old,' said Bahedi, 'and Nagim had to per-suade him a little.' With the end of the gazelle hunt still all too vivid in my mind, Bahedi's choice of words was a little unfortunate, and I had a brief and unpleasant picture of Nagim using his razor-sharp knife as a persuader.

We spent the rest of the day and the following morning rushing around Tamanrasset, taking on fuel and checking the vehicles while Moustaffa organised food supplies and Bahedi arranged our travel permits with the police. I thought we should never be ready, but by three in the afternoon we were once again driving out of Tamanrasset, this time on the main road south to In Guezzam and the Niger frontier. Hamed, Moustaffa and the food supplies were in one vehicle; Bahedi and I were in the other, with Nagim driving.

After a few kilometres we left the main tarmac road and took a short-cut to Amsel. Akali lived in one of a cluster of comparatively new stone and clay-rendered houses in a dusty and litter-strewn part of the village.

'These are all new houses?' I asked Bahedi, who waited with me in the vehicle while Nagim fetched Akali.

'The government built them to settle the Tegehe-n-Efis. Some time ago, now.'

'Why is there so much litter?' I asked, knowing that as a rule Tuareg were meticulous about its disposal.

'It's the military. They've got some rest-houses or something here, for their own people. They always makes a mess.'

Akali was an unusually large, lumbering man, bigger than Sid Ahmed in Mertoutek, and walked with a heavy, slightly rolling gait. He wore a pale sky-blue *gandoura* and a light mauve veil, and carried his bed-roll of blankets under his arm. Pastels may have been the current fashion, but I thought they looked a touch effeminate on such a big man. Akali's eyes were tired and slightly watery, and I put him at about seventy. Bahedi said he was sixty-five and later Akali himself told me he was fifty-five. It was not that he was lying; like many Tuareg, he had probably just lost track of the years. When we were introduced he struck me as being rather stiff and formal and, I suspected, just a little nervous, addressing me as '*Monsieur*'.

After we had driven for about an hour down a network of *oueds* draining out of Ahaggar to the south-west, Akali stopped us by a large rock outcrop to show us some prehistoric rock engravings of giraffes and ostriches. In the light of the lack of interest in rock art shown by Mokhtar and El Mouden, Akali's attitude to the engravings was interesting. He told me that they had been drawn by the ancestors of the Tuareg, people called the Ag Arussi, a name I had never come across. None of the others could throw any light on it. It crossed my mind that 'Ag (son of) Arussi' might be just the sort of name the Tuareg might have given to the Russians, who had spent a few years engaged in mineral exploration in the region shortly after Independence.

One of the best Russian (or, more correctly, half-Russian) stories I had come across in Ahaggar was told me in 1969 by Beh ag Ahmed as we were riding on camels from Tamanrasset to a big Tuareg wedding in this area. 'It was during the Six Day War,' he said, 'and the Egyptians wanted to garage their MiGs in case the Israelis got them. Algeria, as an Arab country, said they could park them at the old Atomic Base at In Eker. So they flew to Algiers, following the coast because they couldn't navigate properly, then turned left over the mountains and picked up the trans-Sahara *piste*. By the time they got over Tamanrasset, two of them couldn't see the *piste* any more because of the mountains. They radioed to Tamanrasset for help, but by then they were almost over Niger. Well, they turned round, but ran out of fuel and crashed near here.'

I asked what happened to the pilots. 'They ejected by parachute,' he said, 'and were picked up by the Tuareg.' I never could find any satisfactory corroboration of the story, but then it was not one that would have been broadcast by the Arab world. I've always had a sneaking feeling it was a tale put about by the Tuareg, who were not at that time too enamoured of either the 'Arabs' from the north, or the Russians who had recently been traipsing around their country. Bahedi said he had never heard the story; Akali, who would have known this area intimately, did say he remembered something about it, but could not or would not be more specific.

Shortly after that we stopped to make camp for the night on the flat, sandy bed of the *Oued* Tigenaouen, next to a garden of about half a hectare in size that had been developed on a stretch of alluvial soil along the bank of the *oued*. The garden belonged to Akali, but was currently being tended by his teenage son Mohammed and a couple of his young friends, who were living in a makeshift shelter nearby.

While the others unloaded the vehicles, I walked with Akali to inspect the diesel pump that drew water from a well in the middle of the *oued,* and to see the garden. Within minutes he had cast off his veil, *chech* and *gandoura* to display a balding head of curly, silver-white hair, and had picked up a hoe to clean out some of the irrigation channels. It was curious to see this old nomad, stripped to his under-shirt, doing work which as a young man he would have regarded with utter contempt. Mohammed, very much a figure of today with his short-cropped hair and wearing a checked shirt, blue denim jeans and trainers, sat on a tamarisk trunk and watched.

Later that evening, Bahedi asked me if I had met Clay.

'No,' I said. 'Who's he?'

'Akali's son, Mohammed. His proper name is Mohammed Ali, so everyone calls him Clay!' Did these Tuareg either know or care that Ali had changed his name from Cassius Marcellus Clay when he joined the Black Muslims, in part because of its slave connotations?

The next morning we were up at first light. The drop in altitude from Tamanrasset of even a few hundred metres was very noticeable: the air, although cold, had lost its sharpness. We loaded the vehicles and were under way before the sun was up, for we had a full day's drive ahead if we were to reach Tin Ghergoh before nightfall. During the first three or four hours it was interesting to observe the subtle changes in vegetation and landscape as we gradually lost altitude and moved out of the mountains of Ahaggar to the flatter desert beyond. The leafier types of acacia gradually gave way to spindlier, thornier and more stunted varieties. In the lower reaches of the *oueds* I noticed one particular bush with bright green, succulent, almost cactus-like leaves that I had never seen in the high mountains of Ahaggar, and pasture became ever scantier before virtually disappearing altogether. The shape and character of the *oueds* changed too: the sand in their beds became finer and the terraces along their banks shallower and finally non-existent – only the finest material was ever carried this far downstream. It was also becoming noticeably warmer. By midday, when we had left the mountains behind us, it was distinctly hot.

We were now travelling across an expansive, undulating plain on which there were no distinct landmarks except for a few low ridges and an occasional rock outcrop. Here and there we came across incipient dunes. Trees, so common in the valleys of Ahaggar, had thinned to no more than a few stunted thorn bushes, and here and there an acacia growing in the shallow depressions which occasionally caught a little run-off water. Before we had left all the trees behind us, we collected the broken branches of a dead acacia and piled the wood onto the roof. Shortly afterwards we stopped for our midday break in the shade of what proved to be the last acacia along our route into an increasingly hot, sandy and all but featureless landscape.

While the others were spreading the carpets under the tree, making a fire and unloading Moustaffa's magic food trunk, I walked a short way into the desert to savour the feeling of space. On my return to the camp, I had almost reached the tree when I noticed a speckled creamy-coloured lizard, about twenty-five centimetres long, prancing about in front of me, like nothing so much as a demented Chihuahua trying to keep a postman at bay. Its large wide open mouth displayed an impressive array of teeth, and it was making a rasping noise which could almost have been a bark. It was most engaging, and I hurried to get my camera. It was still there when I returned, prancing and 'barking' ever more frantically. With nothing to indicate the scale, it would have made a tremendous photograph – a real live fighting dragon, rearing up on its hand legs and breathing everything but fire. I was crouched scarcely more than its length away with my camera poised, each tooth in focus, when the picture in the viewfinder went black and an almighty thud shook the ground. I almost toppled over in shock, and looked up to see Nagim standing over me, an acacia trunk in his hand and a grin on his face. The dragon was pulverised into oblivion.

'It's even more deadly than the horned viper,' Nagim said, quick to explain his intervention. 'It's called *emekwer.*'

I was surprised. I knew there were two species of lizard in Ahaggar that were edible, but I had not thought there were any deadly ones. 'Does it kill many people?' I asked as I got up and recovered my composure.

'No, because it normally runs away. It only attacks when cornered.'

'With two vehicles on one side and me on the other, perhaps that's how it felt.'

'Perhaps,' said Nagim nonchalantly, apparently not unduly surprised or concerned. 'But even if it had attacked you, it has difficulty getting a good bite. The teeth are set too far back.'

I felt sorry for the lizard. The tree had probably been its domain for years. All we were doing was passing by.

We had planned to be on the Tassili-ta-n Tin Georgoh that evening, but as the afternoon wore on our progress became slower and slower, as we got stuck in one patch of soft sand after another. Occasionally the stuck vehicle got out under its own steam, but more often we had to shovel away the sand, lay sand-ladders under the wheels, and put our shoulders to it. In this way we would gain perhaps ten or twenty metres. The process was then repeated, sometimes as many as a dozen times to gain a mere couple of hundred metres. It was hot and exhausting work, but there were no signs of short temper and no attempts to lay blame, either on the drivers for choosing the wrong passage or on Akali for bringing us on a questionable route. The only signs of tension, which had been building up all day, were exhibited by Akali. On several occasions he had shown flashes of autocratic bossiness and cussedness, usually over such trivial issues as the positioning of a carpet at lunch, or how long we should rest at midday. I gathered from Bahedi and Nagim that he had also had something to say about the attitude and lack of respect of young people – by which I took it he meant Bahedi and Nagim!

Late in the afternoon, as we took a rest after one particularly strenuous 'dig-out', I asked Bahedi what was troubling Akali.

'It's very difficult for him,' he replied. 'He hasn't been here for fifteen years, and he doesn't recognise it. It's all changed.'

'It's changing all the time,' I said. 'These dunes are alive. They can move quite a distance in no time at all. You know that.'

'I do. But he was *the* great guide. Everyone knows him as that. Not recognising so much has been a shock to him. And I don't think his eyes are too good, either.'

'He's losing face in front of the youngsters?' In Akali's case, the Tuareg's inherent respect for old age was coming up against an irresistable opportunity to settle a few old inter-generational scores.

'Precisely. That's why he's behaving the way he is. Trying not to admit it makes it all the more difficult. If he can get us to the well at Tin Ghergoh, it will be better.'

'But we don't *need* the well, do we?'

'No, we've got enough water. But for him it's crucial that he find it.'

'Is that why he was reluctant to come?' I recalled Nagim's comments about having to persuade him.

'No, that wasn't the reason,' said Bahedi. His face broke into a wide smile. 'He thinks that our friend Mokhtar ben Mokhtar, "Louar", is after him!'

'You're kidding!'

'I'm not. He thinks that because he is the most famous guide for the area, Mokhtar wants to kidnap him and make use of him.'

'That's ludicrous. Mokhtar doesn't need guides — he seems to be the one person who does know his way around. And if he did, it certainly wouldn't be Akali!'

'Yes, but Akali hasn't worked that out yet. He really is scared, you know.'

I looked over at the big man. He was leaning against Hamed's vehicle, his shoulders slouched, getting his breath back after the recent struggle with the *fesh-fesh*. Remembering my own fears of only a few weeks before about returning to this country, I felt a wave of sympathy for him. It was easy to understand how similar fears and anxieties, compounded by the presence of a younger generation snapping at his ankles, could have taken hold of him. Like Bahedi, I could see that we had somehow to ease him off his high horse, bring him down to earth, allow him to save face, and then humour him. But the time was not yet right.

Soon afterwards we decided to call it a day. We couldn't see the Tin Ghergoh mountains through the afternoon haze, but knew they were not far away. We were all exhausted, and it was plain we would not get across the remaining patches of sand before dark. So we literally downed tools, and made our camp on a flattish area of dune sand.

Later that evening Bahedi and I were talking about Akali again.

'Did you know that he was the guide that found Thatcher?' Bahedi asked casually.

'No! How incredible.'

'You should talk to him about it.'

I went over and sat beside Akali. During the course of the day I had managed to persuade him to call me *Monsieur* Jeremy instead of just *Monsieur*; another day, I thought, and we would get rid of the *Monsieur* too.

'Bahedi tells me it was you who found Mark Thatcher,' I said to him.

'No, that's not quite true,' he said, clearly pleased to be singled out. 'The guide who actually found him on the ground is dead now. I was the guide in charge of the operation. I was in the plane with the *gendarmes*.' We were all now listening to him, and I could see he was enjoying the attention.

'Tell me the story,' I prompted. 'Where did you find Thatcher, and why had he got lost?'

'It was back in the seventies, about twenty-five years ago. I didn't know anything about it until the *gendarmes* called me. Everyone was there, in Tamanarasset.'

'Where had Thatcher gone, though?'

'On the *piste* to Tin Zaouatene. Well, there is no single *piste*. There are about four different routes, spread across quite a wide area; one is more sandy than the others.'

'And that was the one Thatcher had taken?'

'That's where we found him.'

'That sounds like him,' I said.

'You know him?' Bahedi sounded a little surprised.

'Good lord, no,' I said. 'Only what I read in the papers.'

'Where is he now?'

'South Africa, I believe.'

'Is that because of his mother?'

'How do you mean?' I asked.

'Well, wasn't his mother a supporter of South Africa?'

'Not officially, but – well, she stood out against the imposition of sanctions on South Africa, and she publicly called Nelson Mandela a terrorist.'

'And her husband had business interests there, too, didn't he?'

Bahedi had considerable knowledge and experience of the world, and it was no particular surprise to find him so well informed. But there was something faintly surreal about hearing Mrs Thatcher's reputation being weighed by the likes of Moustaffa and Nagim, who both joined in to add their party pieces, in the middle of the Sahara.

The next day, in the cool morning light, we could see clearly the dark, purple line of Tin Ghergoh along the length of the horizon ahead of us, no more than twenty-five kilometres away. As far as I could make out from the maps, Tin Ghergoh, like all the Tassili ranges, was a plateau twenty-five to thirty kilometres in width running for about a hundred and thirty kilometres north–south, its highest points not much more than a couple of hundred metres above the plain we were crossing. Geologically speaking, it was a much more 'mature' version of the Tassili-n-Ajjer on the other side of Ahaggar, its scarp worn down from perhaps a thousand metres to a tenth of that by hundreds of millions of years of erosion. The sight of it lifted our spirits, and we expected to be on the plateau within an hour or so. The fact that the first patches of sand we encountered were firm gave us even more encouragement.

We had not driven much more than a few kilometres when we passed a small heap of sand about thirty centimetres high, a little less than two metres long and about a metre wide, from which a few bits of woven matting protruded. It looked as though it might once have been some sort of temporary shelter. But that was not all. Beside it was a large tin mug, standing upright and three-quarters filled with sand, and a small wooden mortar, the type known to Tuareg as *akabar* or *takabart* which they customarily used on their trading expeditions. Beside the mortar was a stone pestle which looked prehistoric – probably picked up from an ancient site and re-used.

'What is it?' I asked Bahedi, as we all climbed down to look.

He shook his head without saying anything.

'Someone's died here,' I said, more as a statement than a question. Then, when he still did not reply, I said: 'Do you think there's a body here?'

'There could be,' he said, clearly reluctant to talk about it.

As we stood about I noticed Akali snatch up the stone pestle and slip it under his *gandoura*. No one else noticed. My immediate instincts were that we should investigate; it would have been the work of a few minutes to clear away the sand. Jackals would have devoured a corpse, but there would almost certainly have been something in the way of identifiable remains. Then I realised that this was the traditional territory of the Tegehe-n-Efis, Akali's descent group, and that if the pestle had belonged to a Tegehe-n-Efis it was probably identifiable by his kinsmen.

It also crossed my mind that perhaps Akali had known of a kinsman who had set out in this direction and not returned, and I wondered whether he had brought us on this specific route in order to search for remains. But the idea occurred only to be at once discounted: there were no tracks to follow, the sands around us were alive and moving, and the chances of stumbling across such remains as these in a vast expanse of undulating, open desert were less than those of finding the proverbial needle in a haystack. Neither Akali nor anyone else said anything. I was surrounded by silence. It was as if we were not meant to have seen the small pile of sand, and it was not for me to ask questions.

Within a few minutes we were on our way, leaving the site exactly as we had found it except for the stone pestle. No further reference was ever made to it, and I still do not know whether it represented the grave of a traveller who had been taken ill or run out of water, or whether someone had just decided for some quirky reason to abandon his matting, mug, pestle and mortar where he had stopped to rest; but I know what I think. It was all very disconcerting, and the discovery cast a cloud over our earlier good spirits.

The passage we were following into Tin Ghergoh ran between two long *seif*-dunes. They were not particularly high, perhaps ten metres at the most, and in places not much more than three. But it was at these low points, which were where we tried to cross them, that we usually hit *fesh-fesh*.

We could now see the scarp of Tin Ghergoh very clearly. It rose about a hundred and sixty metres above us, much of it covered with banked-up sand, so that the rock did not actually protrude until near the plateau summit. At intervals of about three kilometres all the way along the scarp, massive rock outcrops rose up from the crest like deeply-crenellated castle battlements, and there were some spectacular rocky pinnacles, piercing the sky like soaring church steeples. It was in the shelters and grottoes at the foot of these 'castles' that I hoped to find prehistoric settlement sites.

We were by now close enough to the scarp to be able to see the fissures and battlements of the 'castles' quite clearly; then the two *seif*-dunes on either side of us converged to form a massive and impenetrable sea of sand. Nagim made a series of probes in the hope of finding a way through, but it was impossible. At this point we were about eight kilometres from the scarp itself, and the sand was piled up against it for as far as we could see in either direction. We finally turned around to retrace our route but keeping close in the lee of the northernmost of the two *seifs,* in the hope of finding a way over it. For perhaps thirty kilometres we followed it, hoping for a break, before reaching the tip of it, like a pointing finger jabbing across the otherwise flat desert surface. Once around its tip we headed back towards Tin Ghergoh, which was now out of sight. Once again, within a few kilometres of the scarp the dunes merged, and we were forced to repeat the exercise. I was beginning to doubt that we would ever get any closer, but Nagim, the eternal optimist and adventurer, was still sure he would find a way. Akali, however, was becoming increasingly irritable. The humiliation of being unable to find us a way into the area in which he had made his reputation as a guide was almost too much for him to bear, and he insisted on telling the drivers which routes to follow.

We followed these 'fingers' of the *seif*-dunes up and down for about four hours, covering almost two hundred kilometres on the ground but actually progressing no more than fifteen kilometres northwards and never getting any closer to Tin Ghergoh. Finally, around midday we spotted a valley that was almost encircled by dunes, but in which we could see a line of acacias and a few tamarisks. Akali recognised it, informing us in his most autocratic and acerbic tone that these were the tamarisks that marked the entry to the well, and that we should have come this way to start with. Not even Nagim had the nerve – or was heartless enough – to point out that we had been following his directions all morning.

The acacias offered the prospect of good shade for our luncheon break, but no sooner had we stopped at a well-crowned tree and begun to unload the carpets and Moustaffa's trunk than Akali insisted that we move to another. He was the 'official' guide, so he reminded us, and he knew the valley. I could see Bahedi and Nagim bite their tongues. We moved to the specified tree, which looked no different from the one we had left, only to find that it was colonised by legions of ants. No one said anything and the carpets were spread out as usual, but I think we all knew how it would end. The ants weren't fierce biters, but the speed at which they explored almost every nook and cranny of our bodies was perfectly maddening. The crunch, I could see, was going to come when we had finished eating. Bahedi, Nagim and I had already decided that because we had lost so much time chasing up and down the dunes it would be wise to forgo the usual siesta – this despite the fact that Akali had made it plain the day before that a siesta, and a long one, was an integral part of his day. From the atmosphere that had built up during the morning it was easy to deduce that he was not about to change his habits today.

It was not a question of whether his stubbornness or the ants would win: that was a foregone conclusion. It was merely a matter of how long he could hold out. In other circumstances we would have enjoyed the funny side, but I think we were all rather embarrassed by Akali's behaviour, and sorry for him. He was like a dinosaur struggling to survive in a new environment. We watched as he placed a carpet in the shade of one of the vehicles, lay down and covered himself completely with a blanket. Occasional movements of the blanket were the only sign that the ants were setting to work. Hamed had retreated behind the wheel of his Toyota, all ready to leave. Moustaffa had made sure that all the food was safely packed away in its proper place. Bahedi and Nagim sat and smoked, swatting at the ants, and I whiled away the time ambling around on the look-out for interesting stones on the ground.

Akali lasted for about twenty minutes, then pushed back his blanket and announced it was time to find the well. No one asked how he had slept, and he made no mention of any discomfort.

It was a short, difficult drive from our resting place to the well, since the approach was clogged with sand. But we got through it, and there it was: a circular concrete rim protruding no more than a few centimetres above ground-level, towards the southern end of an open area of flat gravel about the size of two football pitches. The gravel was completely encircled, except for the narrow entrance through which we had just made our way, by high banks of sand that looked as though they might sweep over and drown the place at any moment.

For some time now we had been aware of vehicle tracks, and we had a pretty good idea to whom they belonged. They were several days old, so we were not anticipating finding anyone at the well, and as far as I was aware Akali had made no further reference to his fear of being kidnapped.

Vehicles had indeed been to the well within the last few days, and given the absence of tourists and that Tin Ghergoh was well away from any normal commercial route, we were pretty certain that they belonged to bandits or smugglers. Moustaffa's sharp eyes spotted the first clue, the remains of a rolled 'joint' not far from the well. The hashish in it was fresh, clear indication that it had not been lying around for very long. A few yards further away I found an empty cartridge shell lying on the ground. Picking it up, I showed it to Moustaffa. 'A *Kalach*,' he said, using the local slang for Kalashnikov and not even bothering to examine it.

'They probably tested their weapons here,' said Nagim, 'firing off a few rounds.'

'Who is "they"?'

'Louar, perhaps. *Trabandistes.*'

'Smuggling what? Cigarettes?'

'That's the big business.'

'And passing them through to the rebels in the north?'

'They say Louar's now linked up with Hassan Hattab, one of the main rebels up in the north, so it's quite likely.'

Bahedi had now joined us. 'That's probably why the military have brought in the helicopter gunships,' he said. 'Hot pursuit.'

As we were talking, a rather bizarre thought struck me.

'You remember our conversation last night about Mark Thatcher getting lost here?' I said. Bahedi nodded. 'Well, those cigarettes are Marlboros, from the Philip Morris outlets in Benin and Nigeria. And do you think they don't know that tons of their cigarettes are being smuggled up here?'

Nagim shook his head. 'We can't tell, but this is probably their main market.'

'I don't see the link between Mark Thatcher and Philip Morris,' said Bahedi.

'Well, there isn't a direct link,' I said. 'It's just ironic that at one time his mother was a paid consultant for Philip Morris – and now their products are being smuggled along the route on which her son got lost.'

'And the cigarettes are financing the rebels!'

'There you are,' I said. 'And she spent her whole time in office denouncing terrorists. It really *is* rather ironic, don't you think?'

Akali had been insistent that we should find the well, to enable him to get his bearings. But he hadn't banked on the sand closing in on it. Rather than offering us a route onto Tin Ghergoh's scarp, the few kilometres between the well and the scarp were now a sea of sand quite impassable for vehicles. We had no choice but to retrace our route and try once again try to find a passage between the unrelenting lines of *seif*-dunes. Nagim, who had now lost all patience with

Akali, took over as the lead vehicle. For two hours we followed him up and down the *seif*-dunes, covering another eighty kilometres while making no more than eight kilometres' headway northwards. At the end of the afternoon, our entry to Tin Ghergoh was still barred. Each time we got within a few kilometres of the scarp, our progress was blocked by mountains of sand. I could imagine how difficult the military would find it to catch bandits hiding out in these mountains: they were all but impregnable.

We had almost decided to call it a day and see if we could reach the scarp on foot in the morning, but Nagim was determined to have one more try. He thought he'd seen a passage that might allow him to make a diagonal ascent of the sand and the scarp. Hamed was to wait in the second vehicle, and follow only if he saw us ascend the scarp successfully. Bahedi and I climbed in with Nagim and set off on what I can only describe as a desperation drive. I had visions of spending the rest of the night digging the Toyota out of *fesh-fesh*.

Nagim attacked the huge bank of sand at an acute angle and at top speed. The sand on the lower slope was firm and we powered forward for about four hundred metres without losing much speed. We climbed almost half-way, to a short level stretch, which enabled Nagim to pick up momentum for an attack on the much steeper top half of the slope. For a moment we seemed to be trapped in the *fesh-fesh*, but we lurched through it at high speed, rocking dangerously, until he was able to swing the vehicle off the sand and onto the exposed rock pavement at the top of the scarp. We had made it onto the top of the plateau. Nagim stopped, and waved to Hamed, a small dot nearly two hundred metres below us. Beyond him the lines of *seif*-dunes stretched away as far as I could see. We waited for Hamed to join us, then drove another four hundred metres along the edge of the scarp to a great sweep of bright yellow sand that took us right up to the front of the big rock 'castle' we had singled out from the plain below.

'Elephants!' exclaimed Bahedi.

'Three! No – look – four!' said Nagim, who had stopped to count the extraordinarily-sculpted pillars of rock that jutted out in front of the 'castle' like a herd of elephants. Vertical fissures in the ancient rock, weakened by intermittent moisture and blasted by sand, had opened into a series of life-like crevices: we could walk behind the elephants' trunks, and squeeze between their legs. A professional sculptor would have been proud of so realistic a work.

We pitched camp on the sand between the elephants and the crest of the scarp, then walked around the elephants. Broken pottery, grinding stones and other such implements testified to Neolithic settlement, and I wondered whether those prehistoric inhabitants had appreciated the exceptional magnificence and beauty of the place as much as we did. Just before dusk Bahedi and I explored the 'castle' – the big rock outcrop immediately behind the elephants. We stood on the highest point and looked across the plateau to the north and to the west, where the sun was setting, a great red ball of fire. We had already lost a day in getting here, which left us with little more than a day in which to explore the plateau.

'Why don't we start there?' suggested Bahedi, pointing to a big 'castle' of exposed rock about eight kilometres to our west. 'Then we could work our way northwards, checking out the "castles" as we go.' We could see several, no more than a few kilometres apart, and each had almost certainly been the site of prehistoric settlement.

'It will be easy driving,' I said. 'Not much more than thirty or forty kilometres and no problems for Akali.'

'We just explore northwards, and come off the plateau at the end of the day.'

I scanned the darkening horizon, counting the number of 'castles' to be seen and excited by what I knew we would find in them. In prehistoric times these 'castles' would have formed a chain of little communities running the length of Tin Ghergoh.

The first rays of sun were touching the elephants' heads as we reloaded the vehicles next morning and headed off westwards to the next 'castle'. We hadn't covered more than a kilometre or so when Nagim stopped. 'Where are the others?' he asked, staring intently into the rear-view mirror. 'They're not following.' Bahedi and I craned our necks round: sure enough, there was no sign of the other vehicle. Nagim turned the Toyota, and after a few minutes we spotted them, about three kilometres away and heading due north. I said nothing, but felt anger begin to boil. We had this one day to explore the plateau. Every minute was precious, not to be squandered on Akali's antics. Neither Bahedi nor Nagim said anything. But I could sense that they too were livid. Nagim pressed the horn a few times, but we knew it was futile. They were now about six kilometres away, and fast disappearing out of sight.

'We'll leave them,' said Nagim disgustedly, restarting the engine and swinging the vehicle back onto our original course. 'They can pick up our tracks.'

We reached the first of the 'castles' Bahedi and I had singled out the evening before. It was not as big as we had expected – most of the outcrop was not much more than about seven metres above the plateau. Obviously the sun setting behind it had made it look larger than it was. It was also heavily eroded, sculpted into weird arches, grottoes and tunnels, and there was little sign of any prehistoric settlement.

We were half-way towards the second of the 'castles' when Hamed's vehicle joined us. Bahedi and Nagim merely waved to Hamed, signalling him to follow behind us. Akali might have wanted some sort of showdown, but Bahedi and Nagim weren't going to give him the opportunity, not yet at any rate.

Our annoyance with Akali was soon forgotten in the excitement of approaching the second of the 'castles'. Even a few kilometres away there was a sense that we were about to enter another world. The first sign that this particular 'castle' had been a place of some importance was a line of large stone tombs running for some four hundred metres across the flat, rocky plateau surface. From a distance, the 'castle' had the profile of an inverted basin, but as we drew closer we realised the reality was different. It was much higher than we had expected, rising to at least fifty metres above the plateau, and it was not a single block of rock but dozens of beehive-shaped stacks, between which natural fissures in the rock had been widened by erosion into dozens of narrow passages and ravines.

The most beguiling feature of this 'castle' was its 'moats'. About two or three hundred metres in front of the 'castle' the rock surface of the plateau gave way to compact sand which sloped gradually up to the 'castle'. Then, when we were close enough to toss a stone at the rock face, we saw that the sand fell away, almost a sheer drop, into deep 'moats' encircling each stack of rock. The 'moats' had been made by the wind funnelling around the stacks and scouring out the sand from their bases. The result was that the original prehistoric settlement sites in the grottoes and shelters at the base of the stacks were completely exposed.

Looking down into one such 'moat', I felt strongly that it would almost be a desecration even to disturb the face of the sand wall. But Moustaffa and Nagim, both of whom needed only to see *Indiana Jones* to complete their archaeological training, had already plunged down the steep sand face. I followed them, aware of the same sense I had had in Ahellakane of entering hallowed territory that had not been disturbed by man since its Neolithic inhabitants had left. It was a humbling experience to walk there looking down at tools, knowing that they had been handled, shaped and used by people who had lived, made love, given birth and died here so many thousands of years ago.

Bahedi and Hamed came down to join us. I think we shared similar feelings of awe and reverence. After a few moments we drifted off on our separate ways. There is a strange force in such places which impels one to solitude, a need to be alone with one's forebears, if only for a short while. Akali remained sitting in the vehicle.

The 'moat' floors were littered with artefacts: shards of pottery, broken grinding stones, quern stones of all shapes and sizes, stone axe-heads and other cutting tools, fragments of necklaces made from ostrich-egg shells and stone, segments of beautifully crafted stone bracelets, and one tool – a perfectly shaped stone 'corkscrew' which left me marvelling at its intricate and immaculate workmanship while wondering what it might have been used for.

As I had expected there were few paintings, and those I found were either fairly 'primitive', or suffering badly from erosion. Most of the rock art, which was not in any case extensive, was in the form of engravings. I was examining one fresco of three beautifully stippled and well-preserved animals – they were some sort of 'big cat', leopards perhaps – and wondering how (and why) they had been executed on a rock face that now could not be reached without some sort of ladder, when I was joined by Bahedi.

'Maybe the ground surface was higher in those days,' he suggested, when I put the problem to him. 'Or maybe they deliberately carved them up there so that no one else could carve over them.'

I couldn't disagree with him. 'You sometimes find both engravings and paintings in the most out-of-the-way places. One wonders what the artists had in mind.'

We left the engravings and walked slowly around the 'moat' at the base of the adjoining rock stack. The gap between the rock wall and the sand face rising about ten metres above us was no more than a few paces, and strewn with stones and small boulders. 'Just look at that,' I said to Bahedi, pointing to the tracks on a little pile of sand that had collected against one such boulder.

'*Tachelt,*' said Bahedi immediately, using the Tuareg name for the deadly horned viper. 'And another over here,' he said, pointing to another line of tracks that disappeared under a small rock shelf.

'They're everywhere.' I began to notice their squiggly tracks on almost every patch of sand. 'They can hide themselves superbly, but not their tell-tale tracks.' The 'moat' we were in was a veritable snake pit, and I suspected the others were too.

'Akali did say that the area was infested with snakes,' Bahedi remarked, as we stepped back from the larger stones under which the snakes were clearly hiding. Here, in this sheltered spot and at a lower altitude, it was evident that the snakes were *not* hibernating.

'Let's hook one or two out,' I suggested, keen to have a look at them.

'Oh no!' Bahedi protested. 'They can jump at you.'

I felt pretty certain the vipers couldn't jump, and that their strike range was limited to less than a metre, but Bahedi was adamant, and so we left them undisturbed and rejoined the others.

None of us knew the name of this place. Again I would have been happy to stay here for days, but again time was pressing. 'You can come back here when you next return,' said Bahedi consolingly. 'And I could bring tourists here, for a week or more. They would be spell-bound, don't you think?'

'They would,' I said. If they felt confident enough to come to Algeria at all. But I was reluctant to dampen his enthusiasm. 'Apart from Louar and the *trabandistes,* it doesn't look as if anyone has been this way for years.'

'Akali says not for fifteen years.'

We left the 'snake-pit castle', as I now thought of it, after a couple of hours and made our way slowly northwards, rather feeling that almost anything else we might find on the plateau was bound to be an anti-climax. There were still surprises in store in the form of rock formations, however – some of the most fantastic I have seen any where in the Sahara. For several kilometres the plateau surface was studded with blocks of rock so undercut by the action of wind and sand that they had been turned into almost every imaginable shape of giant mushroom, ranging in height from perhaps three metres to as much as ten or fifteen. Some had been so completely undercut that the mushroom 'cups' had toppled over and now lay awkwardly on the plateau, with their strata running in the wrong direction in an uncomfortable sort of way as the process began all over again. Nagim singled out the largest 'mushroom' we had yet come across for our midday stop.

'Eight metres, maybe ten in places,' I called back to the others, as I paced out the width of the rock overhang under which we had parked both vehicles. 'And not a bad place for bandits?' I suggested to Bahedi, thinking of Louar's men and whoever else might be lurking in this vast desert.

'You could hide an army here,' he agreed.

'Easily. A dozen vehicles and several hundred men under this mushroom alone.' I thought how useless the gunships at Tamanrasset's airport would be in this terrain.

Moustaffa had already made a quick reconnaissance of the shelter in the 'stalk'. Like almost all the others it had been the site of extensive prehistoric habitation, with pottery shards and stone artefacts littering the ground, and rough engravings on most of the inner walls.

We had planned to stop for only a short while, but after we had eaten Akali took himself off to another mushroom for a siesta. Nothing had yet been said about his 'deviation' earlier in the morning.

'If I had tourists with me, I'd have to talk to him,' said Bahedi.

'It doesn't matter.' His behaviour, although irritating, was also very sad. 'We're not in a hurry, not after what we've seen this morning. And anyway, I wouldn't mind wandering around on foot for a while. There are a dozen mushrooms within ten minutes of here.'

Moustaffa came with me. He was very good company, being not only unusually and genuinely interested in the region's prehistory but also a very intelligent and engaging young man. I thought that if Bahedi ever got his tourism business going, Moustaffa would be a key asset. By the time we got back to 'our' mushroom, we had walked about six kilometres in the heat of the day and checked out about fifteen potential sites, most of which showed signs of habitation.

We drove on northwards. As had happened before, by late afternoon we had become blasé, disinclined to stop the vehicles to investigate a mushroom or 'castle' unless it appeared to be something out of the ordinary. We had also been working our way back towards the scarp, for we had to find a way off the plateau before dark.

With only an hour of daylight left, Nagim stopped on a promontory that gave us long views along the scarp in both directions. If we couldn't find a way down here, we would have to spend another night on the plateau. We parted company to investigate on foot. Nagim and Moustaffa set off in front of us, while Hamed and I headed off southwards; Bahedi, who had contrived to be with Akali, headed north.

About an hour later, we knew that the only possible route was one Hamed had spotted a kilometre or so to the south. He had gone on ahead of me, and walked to the bottom of the scarp. He was confident that we could get the vehicles down, but it was now too dark to risk it, so in the fast-fading light we decided to drive nearer Hamed's find and make camp for the night on a wide sweep of sand just under the crest of the scarp.

'I've had a long talk with Akali,' said Bahedi, as he climbed back into the vehicle. 'He wanted to apologise.'

'What did he say?' asked Nagim.

'Frankly, that he's lost it; that the whole journey has been a shock – he just doesn't recognise places. Everything has changed. And his eyesight isn't up to it any more. He realises he shouldn't have come.'

'That's good,' I said. 'Getting that off his chest will make him feel a lot better.'

'I think so too,' said Bahedi. 'I told him we understood how difficult it had been for him – that we didn't need him as a guide, and just wanted him to enjoy the journey.'

Nagim laughed. 'So he doesn't think he's going to get kidnapped now?'

'The subject wasn't raised,' said Bahedi with a smile.

As we unloaded the vehicles, I watched Akali carefully. Maybe I was imagining it, but he seemed to be sprightlier in his movements. He was certainly making a considerable effort to be more chatty and friendly with everyone, even to the point of helping Moustaffa peel some potatoes. Within minutes I could sense that the relationship between Akali and the two he had perceived as his chief antagonists,

Bahedi and Nagim, was reverting to the sort of joking and gentle teasing that traditionally expressed a friendly recognition of the seniority of age.

Bahedi, Nagim and myself were soon settled on the blankets sipping tea. Moustaffa was working on the stew, Hamed was kneading the flour for the *tagella*, and Akali was busily rummaging in his blanket role, looking, I think, for a change of veil. I was too preoccupied watching the last vestiges of light disappear from the lines of dunes beneath us to follow the conversation between Akali, Bahedi and Nagim at all closely, but gathered that Akali had been pontificating about laxity in the observance of Islamic practices. I presumed Nagim and Bahedi were the butts, for my attention was suddenly caught by Bahedi asking Akali a question about Mecca. Akali gave a noncommittal grunt, and to my utter amazement Bahedi said, 'I'm thinking of going there next year and making the *haj*.' I could see that Nagim, sitting with his knees up and his head hunched forward, was trying to restrain his laughter, while Bahedi was holding his left hand outstretched towards me as a signal to keep quiet. Akali could not have failed to hear Bahedi's remark, but he didn't rise to the bait and continued to busy himself with his sleeping roll.

'What on earth were you on about with Mecca?' I asked Bahedi a little later, when Akali was out of earshot.

'I'm just humouring him,' said Bahedi. 'He's become so pompous and self-righteous in his old age. Haven't you noticed?'

'Only that he says his prayers regularly.'

'Ah, there are always little digs. It wouldn't be so bad if he had always been a religious man.'

'Hasn't he?'

'Oh, no. He was quite a joke when we were young. There was a story – I don't know how true it was – that another man was messing about with his wife. By the time Akali found out, the man was living up in El Golea, a thousand kilometres away. Well, Akali borrowed the money to buy a ticket on the bus – you remember the bus?'

'Indeed I do. I went on it myself, once.'

'Well, he went up to El Golea, found the man, and beat him up.'

'And what happened?'

'Nothing. He just got back on the bus and came home. That was it.'

'And the wife?'

Bahedi shrugged.

Later that evening, just as we were about to turn in, Bahedi murmured to me: 'Tomorrow, when we are all together with Akali, you must ask me what Claudia thinks about my making the pilgrimage to Mecca next year!' We both started to laugh. The idea of Bahedi becoming a *Haj* was just so unlikely.

'I'll do nothing of the sort! If you want to rag Akali about religion, you can count me out. Although I think I might have to mention to Claudia that you have been giving it some serious thought. Travelling in the desert has that effect on people, you know.'

'Don't you dare!'

That night, we were a little later than usual settling for the night. Each chose his own spot, so that our six bodies were spread across about fifty metres of the gently sloping sand. The night was calm; there were no clouds and no moon, and I gazed at the magnificent canopy of stars for a while before falling asleep.

I was awakened at about two o'clock. For a second or two I wasn't sure what was happening, but as soon as I pushed back a blanket the blasting force of a sandstorm hit me, the sand grains stinging my face viciously. As I raised the blanket, the wind tried to rip it from me and I was showered with what felt like bucket-loads of sand. I managed to keep my grip on the blanket and pull it around me with the rest of my bedding. The wind was tearing into everything, making a strange drumming noise. Still there was no moon, and I saw no torch-lights and heard no calls from the others. No doubt we were all battening down under our covers in the teeth of the onslaught. As I lay there, clutching my bedding closely so that it would not be torn away, I could feel the weight of the sand piling up against me. I wriggled every so often to make sure I wasn't being buried alive.

The storm continued for the rest of the night, easing every once in a while, but only to return with a vengeance. It was exhausting just to lie there under the blankets, concentrating on holding on to them and breathing. No matter what I did, the sand crept relentlessly into my ears, my nose, my mouth.

With the first light of dawn, the storm stopped almost as quickly as it had begun. As I pushed back the blankets, sand streamed onto my neck and down into my clothes. I looked around, wiping the sand from my eyes, and trying to take it all in. Sand was everywhere: piled up against the vehicles, food trunks and jerricans, and almost completely covering the bodies of the others. They all still seemed dead to the world, except Moustaffa, who was making a fire and boiling water. We gave each other a wave, as if to acknowledge that we had survived. As I stood up, sand poured out of my blankets, my clothes and my hair. Trying to comb it out produced as much hair as sand. I walked over to the fire with that strange sensation of having just stepped on to land after a long sea voyage.

'How are you?' Moustaffa was already pouring the water into the coffee pot.

'What a night!'

'Is everything all right?'

'Yes, I think so. But I had left the food trunk open! I managed to get it closed.'

As he poured coffee for us both, I noticed a makeshift bandage around his left hand.

'What's happened there?' I asked.

'A scorpion got blown into it.'

'You're not serious? Let me see.'

As he unwound the two turns of ripped shirt, he explained that he had been trying to close the lid of the food trunk when he felt what he thought was a piece of stick blow into the palm of his hand.

'And it stung you?' I asked, looking at the puncture-mark, and a slight cut in the fleshy part at the base of his middle finger. 'Is it still sore?'

'A little, but I was able to cut it open and suck out a lot of the poison.'

'How far up your arm does the pain go?'

He touched his biceps. 'It's easing off now. I'll be all right.'

Happily, I have never been stung by a scorpion, but I believe the pain of it varies considerably, according to the species, how much poison is injected, and the state of health of the victim. Moustaffa was young and pretty fit, and if he had sucked out some of the poison he was probably in for nothing more than a painful day. But I thought it would be wise to put a proper dressing over the wound. I also gave him some mild painkillers.

'It doesn't say they're good for scorpion bites, but they are quite good for headaches and general aches and pains. They might help.'

★

We must have resembled a bedraggled army emerging from its bomb shelters. Everyone looked a little shell-shocked, but apart from Moustaffa no one was the worse for wear. By the time we had checked the vehicles and shaken the sand out of everything, we were later than usual in getting started. At least I now knew how sand dunes could grow and move so quickly; on our small patch alone, several tons of sand had been 'rearranged'.

The route Hamed had spotted was easier than we had expected, and we were off the plateau in about ten minutes. The drive back to Tamanrasset was straightforward – we simply followed a north-eastwards passage between the line of *seif*-dunes until they ended, then headed to the right until we picked up our original tracks.

We stopped for our midday break at the tree where Nagim had killed the lizard. I wondered when Nagim and Bahedi would raise the subject of Mecca. They had both been laughing about it like schoolboys all morning. There wasn't long to wait. We were sitting on the blankets, waiting for Hamed to make tea, when Nagim asked Akali if he didn't think Bahedi's idea of making the *haj* next year was a worthy one.

Akali was nobody's fool. He had clearly anticipated that the ragging would be resumed, and he had his answer prepared. He appeared to think for a moment and then, without turning to Nagim or even looking up from the boot he was lacing, said: 'I can't imagine Bahedi making any worthy contribution to religion beyond taking a copy of the Koran and cutting a hole in the middle of it in which to hide the whiskey for his tourist friends.'

Everyone, Bahedi and Nagim included, burst out laughing, quick to recognise that Akali had had the best of that round.

Shortly after our stop for lunch, Nagim spotted a lone gazelle some way ahead of us. The nearest safety, a low rocky ridge, was a kilometre or so to the left. When he saw us the gazelle put his ears back and bolted. Nagim, foot down, tore across the gravel plain to cut him off. Hamed's vehicle, in which Akali was travelling, took no part in the chase. It seemed to me from the outset that the gazelle had a head start, and he duly made the high ground a couple of hundred metres ahead of us. When we rejoined Hamed, Nagim got out to check the radiator. As he did so, Akali also stepped down, and I heard a violent exchange between them in which Akali did most of the shouting.

'What on earth was all that about?' I asked Nagim when he got back in. 'Doesn't he approve of hunting with vehicles?'

'Oh, no. It's not that. He was saying that I didn't know how to hunt properly, and that you shouldn't chase a gazelle on the diagonal.'

'Why not?' I asked. I couldn't understand it. 'Surely, the quickest way to cut it off is to take a diagonal.'

'Of course it is. What does he know about vehicles? He was just wanting to have a go at me.' Whatever Akali had said had got right under Nagim's skin.

A few miles further on, we came across three more gazelles. Nagim took up the chase, with Hamed's vehicle following slowly behind. When one gazelle broke away from the group, Nagim went after it, and Hamed set off after the others. The chase lasted almost half an hour and took us many kilometres back over the route we had already covered. The outcome was another dead animal strung up on the back of the vehicle. When we eventually found the others, about fifteen kilometres further along our route to Tamanrasset, Nagim drew up alongside Hamed to show off his kill.

'What happened to yours?' he asked.

'They got away,' said Akali. 'We've just been waiting here for you.'

'I'm not surprised,' said Nagim, who clearly felt that he had more than proved a point.

We drove on without stopping until we reached Akali's garden in the *Oued* Tigenaouen, just two hours short of Tamanrasset. It was late afternoon by the time we got there. Clay, his younger brother and a group of friends were waiting for us.

I didn't hear what was said, as I was fiddling with a film in my camera, but the picture didn't need words. In front of Nagim, Akali opened the back doors of Hamed's vehicle, pulled out a skinned gazelle, and gave it to the boys.

Touché, I thought. For an obdurate old dinosaur, Akali had had a very good day.

14

Atakor
un terrain abandonné

THERE WERE NOW only three days before I must leave Algeria. I felt I would like to pay my respects to my old friend Khabte's widow Tebubirt, who lived at Tagmart, a little Dag Rali village some forty kilometres from Tamanrasset, as did her younger son, El Boghari. The elder, Abdullah, whose wedding I had attended thirty years before, lived in Mali.

I also wanted to see the high central mountains of Atakor once more, and to visit some of the Dag Rali camp sites I had once known so well. It was a trip I had been postponing quite deliberately. Since my return I had heard on all sides that these mountains were now deserted: the Dag Rali had abandoned their semi-nomadic camps to congregate in the little villages in the foothills of Atakor – Hirafok, Ifrak, Terhenanet and Tagmart – venturing back into the mountains only occasionally to graze their herds if the pasture was especially good. I had so far felt reluctant to court the nostalgia-laden sadness such a return to the past must induce.

The Assekrem *circuit* is a *piste* which makes a loop of three hundred kilometres or so through the high mountains of Atakor. In the past it would have been possible for Bahedi to drive me around it, but the *piste* was now in such disrepair as to be almost impassable in its northern sector, even with four-wheel drive. Instead, our plan was that Bahedi should drive me up the eastern side of the *circuit* as far as Assekrem, the high plateau in the centre of Atakor on which the French priest Charles de Foucauld had built the hermitage in

233

which he lived for much of the six years prior to his murder in 1916. Bahedi would return to Tamanrasset while I spent the night in the tourist rest house at Assekrem. The next day I would walk across the mountains to the Dag Rali village of Terhenanet; Bahedi would drive up the western side of the *circuit* and meet me there, and we would return to Tamanarasset by way of Tagmart

We left Tamanrasset at about eleven in the morning. The *piste* was so bad that for much of the time we crawled along at little more than walking pace. But we were in no rush, and I wanted to absorb every moment of the day. This terrain was stamped indelibly in my memory. I had traversed it alone so many times: on foot, on camel, during the heat of the day and through moonlit nights.

By lunchtime we had crossed the plain to the north of Tamanrasset and climbed onto the lava-strewn middle plateau of Atakor as far as Afilal, one of the biggest *gueltas* in Ahaggar, where rock pools, little streams of running water, sandy beaches and lush green vegetation meander for several kilometres between bare, black lava flows. It was an ideal spot in which to enjoy the picnic of rice salad, fresh lettuce and beetroot, tinned tuna, hard-boiled eggs, fresh baguettes, oranges – and, of course, tea – that Claudia had provided.

I saw Afilal for the first time in 1964, on the second day of the first journey out of Tamanrasset I made. I had bought a camel, and the two of us set off on a trek that was to take me more than a thousand kilometres through Ahaggar. I had stopped at the mouth of the *guelta* to hobble my camel, and suddenly I heard a voice behind me. Sitting on a rock a little further down the valley was a young man. He stood up and waved, and I could see that he was supporting himself on a home-made crutch. His name was Elwafil, he told me; he was the first Tuareg nomad I had ever spoken to. His French was good, his voice high-pitched and perpetually on the edge of laughter. He told me he had been bitten on his big toe by a horned viper, and was on his way to Tamanrasset for treatment. There was no dressing on the wound, and it looked nasty. I offered him my camel and my company, but he declined both, assuring me with optimism and good humour and the greatest politeness that he would get there quicker without us. Undoubtedly he was the better judge of camel flesh: some weeks later my beast was drowned in a flash flood, and the story spread quickly through the Tuareg camps. When I got to Hirafok, there was Elwafil, who greeted me by enquiring whether I had yet learnt to swim! His toe was much better.

Bahedi and I left Afilal and began the steep roller-coaster climb into the heart of Atakor. In this part of Ahaggar there is no sand except in the beds of the *oueds,* just ancient granites and lava of almost every conceivable shape and type. The *piste* twisted and turned between lava pillars, some like giant cathedral organs fallen silent but waiting to bellow their sound heavenwards. On all sides huge plugs of lava – here phallic, there almost needle-shaped, elsewhere more like sugar loaves – reached skywards, each inimitably contorted as it was extruded from the bowels of the earth in a molten state, like tooth-paste squeezed from a tube. Atakor was still as spellbinding as the first time I set eyes on it.

The last few miles of track up to Assekrem are steep, zigzagging up to a col a few hundred metres below the summit. When I first climbed up here it was to find nothing at the top but a small, flat area, less than half the size of a football pitch, which served to park the camels or baggage of passing Tuareg while they climbed up to visit the various *Frères* who succeeded Foucauld in his hermitage; during the difficult drought-ridden years following Algeria's independence, the *Frères* gave much help to the local Tuareg.

Now the parking lot was almost entirely covered by a square, stone-walled compound enclosing two stone block-houses, refuge for tourists and other more specialised passers-by, built and run by the *daira* or municipality of Tamanrasset. Bahedi found the caretaker, who gave me the key to the lower block-house. On its concrete floor were ten mattresses, each with a hard pillow and three neatly folded blankets. No one else was staying there, and I tossed my rucksack onto one of the mattresses opposite the door.

Bahedi and I spent ten minutes checking our arrangements for the next day and transferring the picnic leftovers into my keeping. I planned to set off at about half-past five in the morning. Allowing for stops, I reckoned to cover the forty-odd kilometres to Terhenanet in good time to meet Bahedi there at about two in the afternoon.

Left on my own, I felt immense excitement at the prospect of trek-king through this incredible landscape once more. I felt very fit, and had been gratified by the way my ageing body had stood the rigours of the past weeks. Forty kilometres would not be unduly difficult.

There were still about three hours of daylight left, and much to do in that time. First I climbed the few hundred metres to Foucauld's hermitage. The old rough-hewn pathway had been smoothed and stepped to accommodate tourist feet, for in the days of the tourist boom the hermitage had been a popular pilgrimage or excursion from Tamanrasset. When I first climbed the path as a young man, I had had to stop frequently to regain my breath; now it was only to turn around to enjoy the stunning views of Atakor.

Foucauld's tiny stone chapel was exactly as I remembered it. I walked inside and examined once again the black-and-white photographs of Foucauld himself, his stone altar and crucifixes, the little library of books and articles. Looking through the visitors' book which lay open on a small table, I saw where Jean and Erica Ziegler had inscribed their names. No doubt the Mayor of Tamanrasset had brought them here. For some reason, I felt I did not want to sign it.

Assekrem is a box-shaped mountain, its summit a plateau about a kilometre and a half long, and the hermitage is on the southern rim of the plateau, overlooking the most dramatic of Atakor's mountains. For me at least, however, the best view is one few tourists ever see, from the northern edge of the plateau. Leaving the chapel, I crossed the stone-strewn plateau to its northern rim. It is a dangerous spot: the plateau literally vanishes into space, where the black lava pillars supporting it end abruptly in a vertical fall of more than a hundred metres into the head of an almost Alpine basin that itself falls away for a hundred metres more. The overall drop is at least three hundred metres.

I stared down into the headwaters of the *oueds* crossing the basin, remembering the *gueltas* and fresh water that had made it a favoured camping-place for the Dag Rali. But the once familiar tents were no longer there. It was deserted, save for a bird of prey circling far beneath me. I sat a couple metres back from the rim, absorbing one of the most magnificent views in the Sahara. In front of me, the bare, mauve-coloured rocks and craggy, broken valleys cascaded down to Arechchoum, which we had crossed on our way to Hirafok and Ideles only a short time ago. Beyond Arechchoum I could see the outline of Tefedest about a hundred and sixty kilometres away. Somewhere there, Mokhtar, Kaouadis, Nama, Sid Ahmed and the others were getting on with their lives. To the left, the mountain of

In Eker reared its shameful head. To the right, further away on the horizon, beyond Ideles, I could just make out the mountains of Tourha, home of Agag, Hamdi and, northwards again, Erza. And beyond that, beyond the horizon, were Amadror, Tamdjert, Ahellakane, Djanet, and the rest of the Tassili-n-Ajjer.

Once again I had come to think of this landscape, its mountains, water-holes and valleys, in terms of the people who lived in it. The Tuareg themselves think and speak thus, of *amadal oua-n-X,Y,* or *Z,* the land of X, Y or Z.

Retracing my steps to the col, I next climbed the squat little mountain which partly blocks the southern prospect from Assekrem, to gain an unimpeded view of the sun going down across the whole panorama of Atakor. I clambered around its small summit to a prom-ontory which jutted out like a crow's-nest on its south side. Wedging myself into a narrow cleft, I stared into the fading light, picking out all the familiar landmarks. The extinct volcano of Tahat, tallest mountain in Algeria, was just behind me on my right. To the left of it, Amjer, then the needle-shaped plug of Ilaman, the rugged granites of Taessa, the sugar-loaf of Oul, the organ pipes of Tidjemaiene, and so many more. Between the jumbled peaks were the valleys that once sheltered the Dag Rali camps in which I had stayed. It was a land I had known so well, one I had come to love and value as though it possessed human and even spiritual qualities.

The Tuareg understand such feelings; indeed, to them they are even more vivid. The mountains of Atakor, like those of the other ranges, are not just physical features with names, to be found (or not) on a map: they reflect the social order and values of the Kel Ahaggar who live among them. They have gender: the more softly-shaped lava volcanoes are female, and accordingly have female names, often beginning and ending with 't' – like Tahat – while the phallic lava plugs, perhaps not surprisingly, are male. They are also related by mythological kinship ties. Mount Tahat, for example, is the wife of Ilaman, the highest and best-known 'male' lava plug, but their mar-riage has not been devoid of jealousies and upheavals. Mount Amjer once quarrelled with Ilaman over Tahat and struck him a heavy blow with his sword, which resulted in Ilaman's 'shoulder' and the eruption of a spring beneath his peak. But while Amjer wooed Tahat to be his wife, Mount Tioueyin was in love with Amjer. In a fit of jealousy over Amjer's refusal to leave his place close to Tahat, Tioueyin flounced off in the direction of Mali, only coming to a stop in her present position alongside the *Oued* Amded near Silet, about a hundred and fifty kilometres to the south-west. Mount Iherhé followed Tioueyin, leaving a depression to mark his former proximity to Ilaman, and on arriving in the *Oued* Amded region began to court her; the small crater to the north of the Silet track known as Tegit-n-Iherhé is the mark left by Iherhé before he finally settled in his present position just behind Tioueyin. These love-affairs and quarrels were more than mere romantic mythological tales: they were a reflection of the lives of the countless generations of Tuareg who had lived so intimately among them.

I had set my alarm for five in the morning, forgetting that the moon would be down by then and it would be pitch dark still. I pottered about for half an hour, eating some bread and salad, drinking as much water as I could so that I should have less weight to carry, and repacking my rucksack. My walk to Terhenanet, a mere forty-five kilometres away, required the barest minimum – the good boots, the trousers, shirt, sweater and trusty storm jacket that I wore; plus the weightier items, four litres of water, three cameras (which I now regarded as excessive), spare films, and the remains of Claudia's picnic; plus spare batteries, a pair of sunglasses, a pen and notebook, an extra pair of thick walking socks, a hat, and my passport.

The freezing night air nipped my face viciously when I opened the block-house door. Instinct told me to walk as quickly as possible to keep warm, but in the darkness this was both difficult and dangerous. Even with my torch, I stumbled frequently on loose rocks, especially on the steeper down-slopes. Come the first light of dawn, I was able to pick up speed and take advantage of a few remembered short-cuts. One which saved me a few kilometres followed the *oued* running behind Mount Ilaman, the most prominent of all the volcanic plugs.

I remembered this valley as nearly always sheltering Dag Rali encampments, and had once stayed here with Elwafil and a large section of his descent group. It was a *oued* that had special memories for the Dag Rali, for it was here they had routed a French column in 1917. I remembered the laughter of an old Dag Rali woman as she described to me how she watched the few French stragglers staggering back through the mountains, reduced to eating *tahlé*, a coarse grass, just like camels. Now the *oued* was desolate, with only the stone surrounds of old camp sites to remind me of the past.

By half-past eight I had covered the first twenty kilometres, to the gorge just before the place where the *oued* flows around the base of Ilaman. Much of the gorge was still in shade, and the water in the small rock *gueltas* carried nearly a centimetre of ice. Here I decided to stop and eat the remains of my food – easier to carry inside me, I thought, for the next four or five hours – so I set to and polished off both boiled eggs, the rest of the bread, lettuce and beetroot and the rice salad, leaving only my two oranges and a little rice for the *moula moula*. This little bird, the equivalent of the English robin, except that it has a white head-cap and tail and black body, is the traveller's companion throughout Ahaggar. I washed out Claudia's plastic containers in the *guelta*, drank as much water as I could, took off my storm jacket and repacked my rucksack. I was feeling very confident. So far the walking was proving less taxing than I had imagined, and I was recognising the terrain almost as if I had been here yesterday. Another twenty-five kilometres would be no more than a pleasant stroll.

I picked up my rucksack, its weight now down to eight or nine kilos, mostly cameras and storm jacket, and eased the straps over my shoulders. Almost as an afterthought, I had a pee. Few things in our lives create indelible memories, but such was the stream of bright red blood I now saw splattering onto the gravel bed of the *oued*. Swinging the rucksack off my back, I slumped down on a boulder next to the *moula moula*, rather numb with shock, and tried to think what might be wrong with me.

I felt perfectly well, and there was not the slightest pain. Pain would have suggested an infection, or at least something tangible. All that blood with NO PAIN was somehow very sinister. It must be hepatitis at least, even cancer. And yet – I felt perfectly fit and well. Clearly, however, I ought to get myself to Tamanrasset as quickly as possible.

The question was, How? I tried to envisage what Bahedi's movements would be. Our rendezvous was for two in the afternoon: I guessed that he would leave Tamanrasset at about nine, stop briefly at Tagmart to let Tebubirt and the rest of Khabte's family know we would be dropping in later in the afternoon, and then drive up to Terhenanet. He would get there an hour or so early, allowing himself time to chat with the people there. If I could get to Terhenanet a bit earlier too, then we could get to Tamanrasset that afternoon, and a few hours might make all the difference if it proved to be something serious.

I had told Bahedi I would walk to Terhenanet by way of what was left of the *circuit*, but that would take me another four or five hours. If I were to turn south of the *oued*'s junction just ahead of me and cut through the mountain range of Taessa, however, I could save as much as an hour, since that route represented the long side of a right-angled triangle of which the *piste* made up the two shorter sides. But I would have to cross the great tongue of ancient granites that was Taessa.

I set off confidently down the *oued*, making good time on its wide valley floor. Just past the junction I heard a dog barking, and saw two women sitting in the entrance of a cave in a craggy little mountain next to Ilaman. They were probably from Terhenanet, spending a night or two in the cave in order to graze their goats further afield. I waved, but only the dog responded. Maybe they felt it would be inappropriate to wave to a strange man, especially one wearing a grey baseball cap.

Further down the *oued*, I came across three loose camels grazing beside a short stretch of cool, fresh water where the *oued* dropped through a series of *gueltas*. In the past, I would have drunk that water without hesitation; now I played safe, and drank what I was carrying. I peed again, hoping against reason that the blood had been a hallucination, but there it was again, and it seemed thicker and redder than before. Still I felt no pain.

By eleven it was hot, and difficult to believe that I had been breaking ice only two hours before. I stopped and ate one of my two oranges. I was now only a kilometre or so away from the eastern side of Taessa. All that remained was to cross the relatively easy ground in front of me, find a route through Taessa and get myself to Terhenanet, and Bahedi would be there waiting for me.

I was so preoccupied with medical matters that it was a while before I recognised the stretch of land immediately before me as one of Khabte's favourite camp sites, where I had spent rather a lot of time with him and his family. As I walked slowly towards Taessa, I wondered when Khabte had last camped here, and looked for little landmarks.

Bahedi had described Atakor now as *un terrain abandonné*, and it certainly felt forsaken. I noticed a few places where tents had once been pitched, and found the very camp site where I had stayed with Khabte. There was nothing left there, and had it not been for a couple of small rock outcrops on which I remembered hanging blankets out to dry after a rain storm, I could not have been sure it was the right place. All the small signs of human habitation – goat dropping, bits of wood, scraps of material – had been carried away by wind and rain. What, I wondered, had brought me to this spot? Until a few short hours ago, I had had no plans to visit this part of Atakor. It was as if the ghosts – those ghosts I did not believe in – had been leading me here. I gazed around nostalgically. On the ground on which I had slept more than thirty years ago there was no mark, no indentation, nothing unusual about it. I looked to where the granite outcrop began a few hundred metres away and remembered collecting firewood there with El Boghari, a young boy of ten, while Khabte sat with his knees folded under him, veil off his face, chipping away at the wood with a little hand axe. That was all part of the division of labour. Tebubirt was in charge of the cooking – always *esink*, millet, and without much milk, for they were times of drought – and perpetually asking Abdullah and El Boghari to help her pound the grain in her deep wooden mortar.

I remembered the people I had known in that camp. Khabte was dead, so too were Tamu, Sidi Mohammed and Hadada, nephews and nieces of Khabte's father Abahag whose tents had been pitched alongside Khabte's. His daughter Fadimata had long since gone to live with a widowed aunt, herself now dead. Abdullah, Khabte's eldest son, was my age and living now in Mali, working for a French tourist agency since the decline of tourism in Ahaggar. His wife Kodda, a new bride when I first stayed with him, whom I remembered as a very beautiful young woman of about twenty, had died (so Claudia had told me) some years ago after a long illness. Tebubirt was now living in a house in Tagmart, with electricity and presumably television, I wondered whether she paid any attention to the country's political troubles. El Boghari, now in his forties, was also living in Tagmart, where he drew an income as a Gardien du Parc. According to Claudia, he had divorced his first wife and married the wife of one of his cousins, who in turn had married the divorced wife – it was, Claudia had joked, the modern-day Tuareg version of wife-swapping. Abdullah had also remarried and his second wife, whom he returned to see once a year, or whenever he could get home from Mali, also lived in Tagmart.

More than a generation had passed since I had camped here with Khabte. Many had died, not all of old age, and others had come into the family; more than that – a whole way of life had changed. Here on the empty, wind-swept slopes leading to Taessa were nothing but memories.

I headed south, following a small *oued* along the edge of Taessa to a rock pool where I had once had an extraordinary row with Khabte. It was midsummer and I was filthy, not having washed for days, and had gone to bathe in the *guelta* – used only to water the animals, I should perhaps point out. The *guelta* was something over a metre deep, and I had not been in it for long when Khabte came rushing towards me, screaming and shouting at me to get out at once. I could not understand what he was bothered about, but luckily Abdullah had followed him and was able to explain. Khabte was afraid that wicked spirits living in the *guelta* would enter my body, make me ill and perhaps kill me. After the three-year prison sentence that resulted from his involvement in the skirmish with former slaves at Otoul, Khabte was terrified lest the *gendarmes* should hold him responsible for my death and put him back in gaol.

Khabte would not listen to either Abdullah or me. Turning on his heel he set off almost at a run in the direction of Tamanrasset, declaring that he would report me to the *gendarmerie*. Abdullah ran after him and assured him that I wouldn't die, at least not yet. I played my part, making a big show of taking a couple of aspirin. Khabte seemed to have faith in aspirin, and asked for the rest of the packet for his '*grippe*'. My survival perhaps proved that aspirin had the power to overcome the Kel Asouf. What a good thing he couldn't see me now – turning urine into blood was just the sort of nasty thing they might do, so here I was, living proof of the power of those evil spirits.

The water level in the *guelta* had dropped and the water was crystal clear, so I could see that there were in fact two rock pools, not one, rounded and smoothed by erosion and connected by a short circular tunnel, like an underwater cave, that had been worn away between them. Light from one pool was reflected through the tunnel into the other. No wonder Khabte had been so worried about the Kel Asouf: such a weird and eerie effect could only be the work of spirits.

It was coming up to midday and my short-cut had served me well, but for the first time I felt tired; I could also feel the beginnings of blisters. I took out my last orange, but decided to keep it until I had crossed Taessa. Taessa, I reckoned, was no more than three kilometres or so wide at this point, and Terhenanet was on the other side: I would be there well before two o'clock.

What I had forgotten was how impenetrable Taessa was in places. I had entered it many times and crossed it once with El Boghari – but a little further to the north. Here, I soon found myself entrapped in a seemingly impassable jumble of granite boulders. The *oued* I had been following plunged into a series of deep gorges that turned back to the south-east; in front of me, to the west, were almost vertical walls of granite, weathered and broken up into huge piles of rock. There were no paths, no *oueds,* not even any defiles through which I could find a way. I had no choice but to clamber, as best I might, through the granite. Had it not been for that darned blood, I could have enjoyed myself. Taessa is probably the least known of all Ahaggar's ranges, simply because it *is* so impenetrable. Its rocks are the oldest in the Sahara. For some six hundred million years they have been exposed to weathering, never covered by the ancient geological seas that formed the rocks of the Tassili and enveloped other parts of the Sahara, or subject to the more recent volcanic eruptions that lap Taessa's flanks. Even the flora that survives in Taessa has a primeval look – and cheetahs still live here.

I was no longer walking but climbing, not just piles of boulders but canyons little less than a hundred metres deep. It took me almost three-quarters of an hour to negotiate the first two canyons, and gain no more than a few hundred metres westwards. As the heat of midday became intolerable, I began to feel the first signs of exhaustion. The third canyon was deeper still, and there was no way around it. My rucksack made the descents more dangerous than they were anyway, so I strung two cameras around my neck, wrapped the third in my storm jacket and stuffed it back into the rucksack, which I flung over the edge. It bounced from one boulder to another, and finally came to rest about a hundred metres beneath me.

Climbing up the other side was equally difficult. Using belt, camera straps, shirt and spare rucksack straps I made a 'rope' about three metres long which enabled me to climb freely and then hoist the rucksack up behind me. In half an hour I had progressed another hundred metres westwards.

One more canyon, negotiated in the same way, and I had reached the summit ridge of Taessa. There were no more canyons – but I had also forgotten that the land fell away by about six hundred metres on the other side, and it took me another half-hour to negotiate the steep, rugged descent. I could not see Terhenanet, but that didn't bother me: I merely assumed I had come out of Taessa a little north of the village.

It was about half-past two when I reached the *piste*: I had spent two and a half hours covering less than five kilometres. I sat for a while on a boulder beside the *piste*. It didn't look as if it had seen much traffic lately. I judged that Terhenanet must be two or three kilometres to the south. I was tired. I finished the last of my water, and was about to eat my second orange, but for some reason thought better of it. My feet had taken quite a battering in Taessa, and I decided to examine them instead. I unlaced my boots, and peeled off my socks. It was not a pleasant sight: large blisters on the balls and heel pads of both feet and the tops of most toes had already burst, and the socks were soaking, though strangely enough my feet were not particularly painful. I threw the wet socks away and put on my spare pair. They were thicker and seemed more comfortable, and soon I began to feel I was getting my second wind. It could only be a short walk to Terhenanet, and probably Bahedi had already decided to drive as far as he could to meet me.

I set off southwards on the *piste*. It was closer to Taessa than I had remembered; but then, I had not been here for almost thirty years. After a kilometre or so the *piste* dropped down from the rock surface to run beside a sandy stretch of *oued* in which there were two distinct sets of tyre tracks. If the *piste* north of Terhenanet was almost impass-able, as Bahedi had told me it was, whose tracks could these be? The Gardien at Assekrem had told me that the Mayor and the Zieglers had returned to Tamanrasset on this side; one set therefore belonged to them. The other set, then, must presumably be Bahedi's, which suggested that I had crossed Taessa further south than I thought. Instead of being a few kilometres north of the village, I was obviously *south* of it. Bahedi was now to my north, and probably beginning to become anxious as to my whereabouts.

I could stay where I was and wait for Bahedi, which seemed rather negative, or I could walk northwards, towards Bahedi but away from Tamanrasset, and unnecessary, since Bahedi, returning southwards, must overtake me at some point. So I decided to walk south towards Tagmart and Tamanrasset, in the expectation that Bahedi would probably pick me up before dark. The distance from Terhenanet to Tagmart was about forty-five kilometres, and from Tagmart to Tamanrasset about forty. If I was now about ten kilometres south of Terhenanet, which seemed likely, I would reach Tagmart by about nine or ten in the evening – assuming that my feet held out. I was still passing a lot of blood, but it still wasn't painful and I still wasn't feeling unwell. I set off southwards again, confident that Bahedi would pick me up before dusk on his way home. I was out of water, but the temperature was already beginning to fall and I still had my one remaining orange.

For the next three hours the *piste* crossed the flat middle plateau of Atakor and walking was relatively easy. By half-past six I reckoned I had covered another twenty kilometres and was probably within fifteen of Tagmart. Then, in the fading light, I heard a motor behind me. I stopped and turned around, staring back across the plateau, looking for the clouds of dust or the lights that would tell me Bahedi was coming. I took out my orange, peeled it carefully so as not to lose a drop of precious juice, and savoured it; I was so parched that I could have eaten half a dozen. By the time I had finished, I realised there were no clouds of dust, no headlights, and no more engine sounds. Were my senses playing tricks with me – or, and perhaps worse, was there another *piste* to Terhenanet further to the west, and I was on the old one? It was possible. And it would explain the sound of the engine. In which case, Bahedi was now to the south of me, at Tagmart, or perhaps even on his way back to Tamanrasset. I suddenly became anxious on Bahedi's behalf; he would be beginning to worry, assuming I had had an accident somewhere between Terhenanet and Assekrem. I just hoped he would not do anything as foolish as notifying the *gendarmerie*. That would get us all into trouble!

But if there *was* a parallel *piste,* why were there two sets of recent tracks on this one – and whose were they?

I now had no choice. I must continue on foot to Tagmart, with my last orange gone, and no water. I had another pee. It was still solid blood, but to my immense relief also excruciatingly painful. At least it wasn't hepatitis or cancer! I must have a bladder or kidney infection, or maybe kidney stones. I'd heard that passing a stone could be unbelievably painful. That was it, I thought. The stone or stones had obviously cut me inside, causing all the bleeding; now they were on their way. It was too absurd. I laughed, and felt much better.

It was now dark, but there was a reasonable moon and the early night air was pleasantly cold – a good night for walking. And my feet, although painful, were still attached to my legs, and capable of more. My only serious worry was Bahedi. All I wanted was to be able to let him know that I was all right.

I carried on following the *piste* in the moonlight, certain that I would soon be in Tagmart and taking a rather amazed pride in the fact that I had covered at least eighty kilometres that day – twice what I normally reckoned on. As I checked my watch – it was exactly eight o'clock – I saw headlights looming over the horizon in front of me. It had to be Bahedi – he had gone back to Tamanrasset, and was now coming up the old *piste* to look for me. Then I realised that the lights weren't moving – perhaps he had stopped for a moment. Then the penny dropped: those were the lights of Tagmart. I had forgotten that the little village now had electricity. In the darkness it was difficult to judge distances, but the lights appeared to be just beyond the horizon, say four or five kilometres away.

Not far; but after another hour following the *piste* towards the lights of Tagmart, I seemed to be no nearer. In fact, the glow was no longer ahead of me, but almost directly to my left. And it gradually dawned on me: these weren't the lights of Tagmart, but the lights of Tamanrasset, still about fifty kilometres away. The horrible truth was that there were no 'lights of Tagmart'. I searched the darkness for the faintest suggestion of light and listened for the sound of voices or the barking of dogs. There was nothing; only silence, and the glow of Tamanrasset's lights on the horizon.

I walked on slowly. For the first time I began to feel depressed, as the reality of my predicament came home to me. I should by now have been at Tagmart. I was still following the two sets of tracks but somehow, for reasons I did not understand, I had missed Tagmart in the darkness. Bahedi was still my main concern, however. By now he would be certain I had had an accident somewhere. It wasn't Tagmart but Tamanrasset I had to get to as quickly as possible, preferably before he set off again at dawn or, worse still, notified the *gendarmerie*. This meant that, without water, I would have to keep walking to the next well, at the village of Otoul, about twenty or twenty-five kilometres on from Tagmart and only twenty from Tamanrasset. Otoul was not far off the main road, where there would be some sort of traffic even in the early hours of the morning. I could be in Tamanrasset in time for breakfast.

I walked as fast as I could for the next two hours, but pain forced me to stop regularly for a pee; I was still passing blood, but no longer overly concerned as to the reason. More worrying now were my feet, which were beginning to become painful enough to slow me down. Even so, I managed to keep up a pace of perhaps four or five kilometres an hour. Everything would be all right if I could get to Otoul.

It was about eleven when things began to go wrong. The moon disappeared behind a bank of cloud at about the same moment as the *piste* more or less came to an end in an area of a broken and rugged terrain of rock outcrops and short, steep-sided little *oueds*. This I knew to be where the middle plateau I had been crossing since leaving Taessa dropped down to the same level as the plain behind Tamanrasset. It was now pitch dark, and with only a pen-light torch it was almost impossible to see where I was going. I was also beginning to feel the effects of dehydration – my tongue began to swell and my mouth to dry out, making it difficult to swallow. I had had no liquids for nine hours, the juice of my orange apart. And my feet were beginning to tell me that they were seriously damaged. I decided against taking my boots off to examine them, realising I probably wouldn't be able to get them back on.

I blundered on in the darkness for another hour. Each time I stumbled against a stone it was as if I were treading on red-hot knives. I had covered little more than a kilometre or so when I found myself in a wide, sand-bottomed *oued*. I gave in to temptation: I stopped by a boulder, scraped a hollow in its lee and lay down. I would rest my body for half an hour, give it a chance to recover a little. And the cloud might have shifted by then, and restored the moonlight.

I had noticed that it was cold, but walking had kept me warm. Now, as I lay in the sand, I could feel freezing air closing in around me. The wind was getting up, too. I buried my head in my rucksack, pulled my storm jacket around me, and forced myself to think of anything except water and drinking.

Within minutes I was asleep. Then I awoke, shivering, and so cold that I could scarcely move. I looked at my watch: it was two in the morning and I had slept for precisely forty minutes. I tried to move, but except for my arms there was not much engagement between brain and muscle. I had stiffened up, and my legs were numb from the cold. I forced them to move, only for a sharp stab of pain to remind me of my feet. I stood up, telling myself there were still more than four hours or so before dawn, and during those four hours the temperature would continue to fall. Suffering was a virtue, I reminded myself – and in any case, I needed to walk to get my circulation going again. At least the cloud had blown away, and there was now enough light from the moon for me to make out my immediate surroundings. But I discovered that walking was no longer a straightforward matter. The pus and fluid in my boots had either congealed, or frozen. My feet were ice-cold and hard, and each movement felt as though it was pulling scabs off. It probably was. I dreaded the prospect of eventually removing my boots.

I forced myself along, one step at a time, counting. After a hundred steps the coagulation in my boots had loosened, and excruciating agony had been reduced to persistent but bearable pain. The terrain was now sandier, which didn't make walking easier. I continued south, knowing that sooner or later I would hit either the main *piste* to Tagmart, or the *oued* Otoul. I reached the Tagmart *piste* first, to find the final confirmation that I had been following the old *piste*: it was lined with pylons carrying electricity into the village. It was then I began to realise that my counting rarely progressed beyond the seventies or eighties. Dehydration, tiredness – probably a combination of both was affecting my brain. That in itself was interesting and gave me something else to think about. It struck me as a good thing, in the circumstances, that my brain should pack up before my legs: those I still needed.

I forced myself to continue walking for a full hour, and I rested again at three, using the concrete base of one of the electricity pylons as a wind-break. A dog would have found it more useful, I thought, as the bitter wind continued to sear through me.

Dogs reminded me of Sidi Mohammed ag Ahmadu, and the time in 1971 when I drove him down to Tamanrasset to make his last caravan to Niger on the back of a lorry: a dog had rushed out at the Land Rover as we passed through Terhenanet, and was nearly run over. I remembered, too, a most heart-rending story Sidi had once told me. Magnificent of face, build and gesture, he was then in his fifties, my age now, and I had a great affection for him. He was tough, both physically and mentally; some of the younger men thought him crazy to persist in his nomadic way of life. He had two children, a son aged fourteen and his daughter, Fadimata, who was still only a baby. I knew he had once had another daughter, Raysa, and when we were sitting together one day, talking about pasture, I asked him what had happened to Raysa. He raised his head suddenly and his eyes bored into mine with an almost frightening look of mingled surprise and anger. 'Who told you about her?' he demanded. It was simply, I said, that I had once heard that he had had more children, in the past. There was a long silence as he stared at the ground, fiddling with some stones. I expected he would get up and walk off with a rough denial, but instead a most piteous expression replaced the ferocity, and his voice shook with emotion.

'We were camped in a place like this,' he said, 'close to here. Raysa wandered off at about five in the evening – at dusk. She wandered off alone. It was winter and very cold, and she wasn't wearing a shirt – she wasn't wearing anything – and she got lost. After she had wandered off into the rocks we realised that she was missing. We searched throughout the night but couldn't find her. In the morning, in the daylight, we soon found her – dead. She had died of exposure. She was about three or four years old. Mohammed, my son, found her body – her brother found her. It was down in the valley over there – not very far away – in the *Oued* Tourtourine. It happened about four years ago.' He looked up, and was smiling. 'After that I decided to have another daughter – Tata was born.'

Again I slept for exactly forty minutes before the cold woke me. Shivering, I struggled up, the pain in my feet even more intense as I began the routine of literally forcing one foot in front of the other as I counted. Thinking of Sidi and Raysa helped take my mind off the pain,

I somehow managed another hour of walking, covering maybe three or four kilometres. A little before five I rested again, again sleeping for exactly forty minutes. It was uncanny and mildly fascinating to see how my body-clock reacted with such precision to the cold. This time it was almost impossible to get going again, but the knowledge that it was only another few kilometres to Otoul and water spurred me on. When the sun came up, I could see the tamarisks in the *Oued* Otoul little more than a kilometre away; the village and well were to the right, on the other side of a low ridge. That last stretch was the most difficult. I snailed my way up the long gentle incline, a hundred paces and then a rest, a hundred paces and then a rest. When I got to the top, I sat down on a boulder. The *oued*, with its well, was in front of me, less than a kilometre away across a flat sandy plain. Music was blaring out from the village just beyond the well.

I was about half-way to the *oued* when I saw a man walking across the plain towards me. He greeted me in Tamahak. My mouth was so parched and my head so addled that I wasn't sure if I could say anything in any language, never mind explain what I was doing and what I needed. He was in his fifties, perhaps a little older, and a former slave. At any other time I would have been determined to find out if he knew anything of the set-to between Khabte and the freed slaves — but now I wanted water, not conversation. What would Khabte say if he could see me now, I wondered? That I was mad, I thought. The man was keen to show me his papers, and one glance told me why: he was a Gardien du Parc, and insistent that I should see what I knew to be Otoul's one and only rock engraving!

'After the well,' I said. My attempts to explain that I had just walked from Assekrem and had been without water since Taessa clearly made no impression. I quite realised why: it must have sounded both incredible and absurd. But he took me to the well.

When we reached the well, my companion's attention was suddenly distracted by something, to the extent that I had to remind him that I wanted to draw water. It was good — if not quite as good as the water I had imagined during the night. I drank almost a litre, slowly, then put another couple of litres into my container. It was not quite half-past seven, and the water felt warm by contrast with the air. When I had finished drinking, I asked what was bothering him. Someone had stolen the pump during the night, he explained.

I thought about it: it made no sense. Things like that weren't stolen here — they could be traced too easily.

At his request I waited by the well while he went off to see someone in the village, presumably about the stolen pump. Returning, he announced that he was taking me to see the rock engraving. I had seen it many years before, and knew it to be of no interest. In any case, I wanted to get to the main road and to Tamanrasset before Bahedi became even more anxious than I feared he already was. Since the story of my walk from Assekrem had played so badly I switched tack, and told him I had injured my leg and needed to get to the hospital at Tamanrasset as soon as possible. That at least matched the evidence of his eyes. He took my rucksack, and led me to the house of a villager who owned an old Land Rover. He had no fuel, but he joined us, and the two of them carried my rucksack between them while I struggled along behind as best I could over the remaining kilometre to the main road. I found it hard to believe that I had now walked between a hundred and twenty and a hundred and thirty kilometres, not to mention the climbing through Taessa, in exactly twenty-six hours.

We were about half-way to the road when a Toyota Land Cruiser came hurtling towards us at high speed, clouds of dust billowing up behind, veiled shouting heads hanging out of the windows like a bunch of cowboys. It passed, roared around in a circle and then drew to a halt beside us, engine still running and the driver shouting excitedly in French.

'You are Jeremy Keenan?'

'Yes,' I replied cautiously, slightly anxious to know exactly who might be searching for me.

'Yeh! *Monsieur* Jerry! It's you! Get in,' he cried even more excitedly as the passenger door behind him was flung open. I found myself being half-dragged into the vehicle. There was no time to thank my two companions from Otoul before we were careering at high speed across the dirt and on to the main road.

I looked around, still with no idea who had picked me up. There were seven or eight of them — two in the front, two beside me, and three or four in the back. They were all veiled, and clearly excited.

'You don't recognise me?' the driver asked, turning around to look at me while somehow keeping the vehicle on the road.

There was certainly nothing about his dress or deportment I recognised, yet there *was* something familiar about his eyes. Who might expect me to know them? I tried to think. Nagim, Hosseyni, Hamed, Moustaffa — I would have recognised any of them at once. Then — 'El Boghari!' It was an inspired guess.

'He knows, he knows!' The Land Cruiser filled with hilarity and whoopee.

I felt a hand from the back touch my shoulder as the driver said, 'That's El Boghari in the back. I'm his brother.'

'Abdullah?' I was incredulous. 'But I didn't think ... You are supposed to be in Mali!'

'I got back to Tagmart yesterday afternoon, just before Bahedi came down from Terhenanet to say that you were lost.'

I didn't know what to say. It all seemed so incredible — far too many extraordinary coincidences.

'These are all the men from Tagmart. We've been tracking you all night.'

'How do you mean?' I presumed he meant that they had been looking for me, unable to believe that anyone could really have been 'tracking' me.

'Bahedi went up to Terhenanet at midday. When he found that you hadn't arrived, he went to Assekrem, only to learn that you had left there before dawn. He then found the women who saw you turning at the *oued*, so he knew you had gone down the other side of Taessa. When he got back to Tagmart in the evening and told us that, I knew where you would be because you knew that country. You stayed there with us!'

'That's right,' I said. 'But surely you weren't actually able to *track* me?'

'It was easy. I knew where you would cross Taessa. We soon picked up your tracks, and your orange peel!'

The way Abdullah was describing it, I rather felt like a general benefactor, having provided the excuse for a magnificent chase and party all over the country. It all seemed incredible, nevertheless.

'But why did you miss Tagmart?' he asked.

'I have no idea,' I said. I was still confused on that score.

'You went right past it. We found where you had slept in the *oued*. That was only about two kilometres from the village.'

'Your dogs should have barked,' I joked. 'Where is Bahedi, now?' I suddenly realised he would not know that I had been 'rescued'.

'He's on his way to Terhenanet again now, but when he passes Tagmart he will hear that we picked up your tracks there.'

'Did he report it to the *gendarmerie?*' I asked, slightly hesitantly.

If I had cracked the funniest of jokes, it could scarcely have provoked more laughter.

'The *gendarmes?*' a voice cried out from the back. 'They get lost when they leave Tamanrasset!' The comment was met with more shrieks of laughter. I got the message. The confidence and ability of these people was unequalled. The desert was still their domain, even if it was now shared with the likes of Louar.

We were in Tamanrasset in fifteen minutes. Abdullah stopped at one of the roundabouts, and the others bailed out. There had been no time to talk to them, only for my profuse thanks and now to say goodbye. Abdullah and I drove on out to Bahedi's *gîte* complex at Hadrian.

Whatever anxiety I might have caused was brushed aside amid Abdullah's joviality and Claudia's relief that I was safe and well. I sat with them for an hour or so in the sun, telling them about my journey, describing how Abdullah had found me, and then listening as Abdullah talked about Tebubirt, his family, and his work in Mali.

We could not get over the extraordinary coincidence that he should have returned from Mali the previous afternoon. After a while, I became too tired to concentrate on what was being said. And I still had to get my boots off. I apologised to Abdullah and hobbled first to the loo, in some dread. To my amazement, there was no blood, and no pain!

'I have the answer for your feet,' said Claudia, as I struggled with my bootlaces. 'It's a wonderful cure.'

'What is it?' I asked. I was fairly certain they were beyond homely remedies.

'Camomile tea. You must put them in a bowl of warm, strong camomile tea.'

My mind was full of *The Camomile Lawn* and Calypso as I eased off my boots and then my socks, which were soaked with blood and pus and had to be peeled off carefully. It was a horrendous sight — two suppurating slabs of meat. I lowered them delicately into the bowl of tepid camomile tea Claudia had provided. It was magic: soothing and cleansing and not one iota of pain. I sat like that, with my feet in camomile tea and drinking iced orange juice by the jugful, until Bahedi returned. I was too exhausted for sleep.

When I saw Bahedi, looking tired and drawn, I felt that the previous night had been worse for him than for me. I at least had been certain that, no matter what discomforts I might have to endure, I was not going to die. He had not. But all was forgiven, my apologies for all the inconvenience I had caused swept aside with professions of relief that I had come to no serious harm, lightened by his inimitable humour.

'You certainly didn't pick the best night for sleeping out,' he said. 'Nagim heard that about forty sheep froze to death at Silet [about ninety-five kilometres west of Tamanrasset] during the night.' I could well believe it.

Claudia had rung the hospital, and they suggested I see a Dr Latreche, who had the equipment to give me an abdominal scan. I showered, put on fresh clothes, and we drove to his surgery. He prodded and probed and scanned my kidneys and abdomen. Nothing untoward was revealed. I might have passed a kidney stone or stones, he agreed, but it was more likely that my kidneys, bruised from all the walking, had just simply started to bleed. It was common in the army, he said. He was more concerned with my feet, covered with deep abscesses which he feared might all too easily become infected. In good French tradition he prescribed a plethora of painkillers and antibiotics which he assured me would get me back to England without risk of infection and without too much pain.

My plane left early the next day.

I slept fitfully that night, and thanks to Dr Latreche's prescriptions was not in too much pain in the morning, though walking was still a major undertaking. Bahedi hated tarmac farewells, and left it to Claudia and Moustaffa to run me out to the airport. It was sad to say goodbye to him, but I promised I would be back again within a few months.

'Not thirty years!' he insisted.

'No more than six months,' I said. 'And that's a promise.'

Moustaffa carried my case and rucksack for me as far as the baggage check-in. After that I was on my own – not easy, as I had to identify my luggage on the tarmac and then carry it to a trolley for loading onto the plane. By the time this was done my feet were throbbing with pain, and I was almost the last to board. I hobbled up the steps at the rear of the plane, leaning heavily on the handrail to take what weight I could off my feet. The plane was crowded, and there was no seating allocation, but I found myself with a choice of half a dozen seats at the back. Not that I minded where I sat. As I looked around, I saw that the last two seats on the port side against the window had been taken out and replaced with a stretcher. Strapped onto it, covered in blankets, was the slight figure of a Tuareg woman. Her face and neck were so thin and emaciated that it was difficult to tell her age – fifty, maybe sixty? I thought of Mokhtar's wife Nama being flown, terrified, to hospital in Algiers. I looked at the tiny face. The big brown eyes were wide open, staring at the illuminated panel above her head. They were the same colour and held the same look of terror as the eyes of Nagim's gazelle, its head left on the desert floor with the eyes staring vacantly up into the pale blue sky.

I found myself in the window seat across the aisle and one row in front of the Tuareg woman. I swallowed a couple more painkillers, sat back in my seat and looked out of the window at the helicopter gunships parked alongside. I closed my eyes, suddenly feeling immensely sad and lonely.

As we lifted off from Tamanrasset's long runway I glanced over my shoulder at the woman on the stretcher. She was immobile, her eyes still fixed on the No Smoking sign above her. I wondered whether she would ever return to her home here in Ahaggar.

We circled over the town and turned onto our northwards course. I had determined not to look out of the window, but I did. I could see from the mountain behind Tagmart all the way across the plateau, up to Taessa and Ilaman beyond. It all looked so tiny, so far away, and so inconsequential.

I lay, fully dressed, on the huge double bed in the Hôtel El Djazair, still known to old Algiers hands as the St George. It was early evening, and the daylight had gone. But I could not sleep, and felt profoundly depressed – just Dr Latreche's antibiotics, I hoped. My flight to London was not until the morning.

Bahedi had faxed to book my hotel room and arrange for a taxi to pick me up from the airport, for which I would be eternally grateful. He had also mentioned an Englishman, Tom Metcalf, who lived permanently in the El Djazair. 'I'll fax him, too,' Bahedi had said. 'He might still be there. If he is, you will find him very interesting.'

The phone ringing beside the bed took me by surprise; so too did Tom Metcalf, for I had forgotten Bahedi's plan.

'Let's meet in the bar at eight,' Tom said. 'It'll be good to have a beer and a chat.'

The idea of a beer (or two) was appealing. I hadn't tasted beer for weeks. I showered, put new dressings on my feet (which looked grotesque), and hobbled down to the bar.

Tom was there already, sitting on a black leather sofa in one of the alcoves.

'You look as if you've been in the wars,' he said as he rose to greet me. He was of medium height, about forty, lean and clean-shaven, with a tough, angular face. He looked what he was – a professional's professional, a soldier by training and now in charge of security for all United Nations personnel in Algeria – and had been living in the El Djazair for security reasons. He was now about to leave – not before time, he said – to take up a post in the Balkans.

He felt like drinking and talking, and so did I.

It was rather more than a beer or two that we drank. We stayed in the bar until well after midnight, by which time my feet felt much better. So too did my intellect, for Tom gave me the clearest and most comprehensive exposition of Algeria's present crisis I had yet heard. It was his job to know who was killing whom, and of course he had access to Algeria's own security networks.

'Did you come across Mokhtar ben Mokhtar in the course of your travels?' he asked.

Louer again, I thought. 'I came across the name a few times,' I replied cautiously. 'Some sort of bandit.'

'You can say that again! He's just about running an army, with the whole country looking for him.'

'Is that why security on the planes is so intensive?'

'Not just planes – everywhere. No one knows what he looks like. Maybe he does have one eye, or maybe that's just part of the myth. Perhaps he did lose it in Afghanistan. No one knows. It could just be glaucoma, of course. You've seen it in the desert. When he was a child, half of them had eye infections.'

I thought of Nagim's meeting with Mokhtar, but didn't mention it. 'How many men does he have?' I asked instead.

'Difficult to tell. You've heard they've just cancelled the Dakar Rally? It's rumoured that about a hundred and forty of them are just waiting somewhere over the border, in Niger or Mali. But that probably includes others. Mokhtar, I reckon, probably has about forty men and vehicles, perhaps more. The vehicles are equipped with geo-satellite positioning, and he keeps fuel supplies buried in jerricans all over the desert, five feet deep because of the heat.'

'That's staggering,' I said

'Sure. But it's a big operation. In the last six months alone he's lifted three hundred and sixty-five four-wheel-drive vehicles out of Algeria. He's even shot down a military aircraft. You don't mess with this guy!'

'What does he do with them all?' I asked. The scale of what Tom was telling me was hard to believe.

'Algeria is the richest country in the region, and it has the sort of infrastructure the rebels down south don't have. He supplies the Chad rebels, and no doubt others, with vehicles and other such goodies. In exchange, they provide him with arms. And then there is the parallel trade – cigarettes.'

'The history of the Sahara has always been written in its trade routes,' I said. 'It seems that nothing much has changed, except the technology.'

'No, probably not. Now it's GSP, night-vision gear, hot-rodded Toyotas, and all the latest arms.'

'What's he up to?' I asked.

'He's at war with the Algerian State.'

'Why? What triggered him off?'

'Who knows? I suspect his family has always been involved in smuggling. His brother apparently got caught and killed by the police some years ago. Maybe it began as revenge for his brother's death.'

'I was in a little desert village yesterday where the diesel pump at the well had been stolen during the night. Might that have been anything to do with him?'

'Almost certainly. Pumps are essential equipment – they need them to get the fuel out of hijacked tankers.'

It was incredible to think that Mokhtar ben Mokhtar's men might have been at Otoul during the night of my walk.

On reflection, however, it seemed that I had been dodging their tracks for most of my journey.

Postscript

At the beginning of February 2001 the Algerian Arab-language newspaper *El Youm* reported that Mokhtar ben Mokhtar had been killed in an incident in the M'sila region, just south of the Hodna mountains – the sixth time his death has been reported in about as many years. From Tuareg I asked to comment on this report the reply was sceptical, the gist of it being that 'phantoms' have their usefulness.

Glossary

(Tk) Tamahak; (Ar.) Arabic; (Fr.) French

ag (Tk)	son of (e.g., Mokhtar ag Bahedi).
Aguh on tohlo (Tk)	vassal descent group of the Kel Ahaggar, traditionally attached to the noble Kel Rela.
Ait Lowayen (Tk)	vassal descent group of the Kel Ahaggar, traditionally attached to the noble Kel Rela.
akabar (Tk)	a type of wooden mortar.
Amenukal (Tk)	the title of the supreme chief of the Kel Ahaggar. It effectively ceased to exist in 1974, in which year the drum (*ettebel*) which symbolised the Amenukal's authority was transferred from his camp to the offices of the Commune of Tamanrasset.
anet ma (Tk)	mother's brother (an important kinsman in all Tuareg groups).
borgne (Fr.)	one-eyed (see *Louar*).
Chaamba	Arab tribe, formerly nomadising in much of Algeria's northern Sahara, and traditional enemies of the Tuareg; pronounced 'Shaambi'.
chech (Ar.)	veil or head-cloth. There are many terms for the Tuareg veil and particular parts or features of it. The *chech* (or *chach*) is known in Tamahak as *echchach*. The term is technically reserved for the white or black manufactured muslin cloth, as distinct from the traditional Tuareg veil (*tagelmoust*) made from Sudanese indigo-dyed cloth. In this book the term *chech* is used to refer to the head-cloth rather than that part of it which may be used to veil the face, which is referred to as *tagelmoust*, a simplification of a more complex range of terms and usage.
contrabandiers (Fr.)	smugglers (referred to colloquially as *trabandistes*).
Dag Rali (Tk)	vassal descent group of the Kel Ahaggar, traditionally attached to the noble Kel Rela.

261

Dakar Rally	a vehicle rally from Paris to Dakar in Senegal, traditionally run in January. Its route over the Western Sahara varies from year to year.
djenoun (Ar.)	evil spirits.
efelehleh (Tk)	a deadly poisonous plant found in parts of Ahaggar: *Hyoscyamus muticus* ssp. *falezlez*.
emekwer (Tk)	a lizard, reputed by the Tuareg to be deadly poisonous.
ened (pl. *eneden*) (Tk)	blacksmith.
erg (Ar.)	sand sea.
esink (Tk)	millet.
fenec	the North African fox.
fesh-fesh (Ar.)	soft sand.
Fulani	a pastoral people, found extensively in the Sahel regions of Burkina Faso and Mali.
gandoura (Ar.)	the Arab kaftan.
Garamantes	ancient population of the Fezzan (Libya).
gîte (m.)	an overnight shelter or lodging, hence a holiday cottage.
grippe (f.) (Fr.)	influenza.
goumier (m.) (Fr.)	Arab auxiliary in the French army.
guelta(s) (pl. *agelman*) (Tk)	natural water-hole.
harratin (sing. *hartani*) (Ar.)	caste of agriculturists; see also *izeggaren*.
Hawarra	ancient Berbers of Tripolitania, Cyrenaica and the Fezzan; possibly the ancestors of the Tuareg.
Hoggar (Ar.)	Ahaggar.
iklan (sing. *akli*) (Tk)	slaves.
Iklan-Taoussit (Tk)	vassal descent group of the Kel Ahaggar, traditionally attached to the noble Kel Rela.
Imenan	ancient noble tribe of Ghat/Ajjer region.
Isebeten (Tk)	ancient vassal tribe of Ahaggar, thought to be the ancestors of the Dag Rali.
Isekkemaren (Tk)	a particular vassal class among the Kel Ahaggar, thought to descend from unions between Arab men and Tuareg women at a time when the northern Tuareg made alliances with Arab tribes or tribes of mixed origin in exchange for certain land rights in Ahaggar.
izeggaren (sing. *izeggar*) (Tk)	caste of agriculturists; see also *harratin*.
Kalach	colloq. for Kalashnikov.
karem (Ar.)	the fast observed in the holy month of Ramadan.
Kel (Tk)	'People of', as in Kel Ahaggar, People of Ahaggar.
Kel Ahaggar (Tk)	literally, the People of Ahaggar (traditionally, the federation of Tuareg tribes and descent groups who lived in Ahaggar).
Kel Aïr (Tk)	literally, the People of Aïr (or Ayr) (traditionally, the federation of Tuareg tribes and descent groups who live in the Aïr Mountains in Niger).
Kel Ajjer (Tk)	literally, the People of Ajjer (traditionally, the federation of

	Tuareg tribes and descent groups who live in and around the Tassili-n-Ajjer).
Kel Amadal (Tk)	People of the Earth (see *Kel Asouf*).
Kel Asouf (Tk)	wicked spirits, sometimes known as *Kel Had* (People of the Night), *Kel Tenere* (People of the Empty Places), *Kel Amadal* (People of the Earth).
Kel Had (Tk)	People of the Night (see *Kel Asouf*).
Kel Hirafok (Tk)	a section of the Dag Rali.
Kel In Tunin (Tk)	Isekkemaren descent group of the Kel Ahaggar traditionally attached to the noble Taitok, but settled predominantly in the Tassili-n-Ajjer, in the region of Tamdjert.
Kel Medak (Tk)	vassal descent group of the Kel Ajjer.
Kel Rela (Tk)	noble descent group of the Kel Ahaggar.
Kel Rezzi (Tk)	immigrant Arab nomads (*Ahl Azzi*) who married into and settled with the Kel Ahaggar.
Kel Tenere (Tk)	People of the Empty Places (see *Kel Asouf*).
Kel Tourha (Tk)	traditionally, Isekkemaren attached to the ancient Tegehe Mellet noble descent group. Also section of the Ait Lowayen who live predominantly in the Tourha mountains and often found in the Tefedest.
Kel Ulli (Tk)	literally, People of the Goats. The term used to designate vassal descent groups, in preference to the term *imrad* (vassal), since it is deemed more in keeping with their predominant economic activity.
khamast (Ar.)	traditional agricultural contract; from the Arab word *khamsa*, five.
louar (Ar.)	one-eyed person (see *borgne*).
méhariste (Fr.)	fast camel rider.
mokhadem (Ar.)	a holy man.
moula moula (Tk)	bird found in Ahaggar.
oued (Tk)	river valley (Ar. *wadi*).
piste (Fr.)	track.
seif (Ar.)	literally, 'sword'. *Seif*-dunes are the knife-edged dunes which form with their axes parallel to the prevailing wind, undulating walls of sand that can be very long (100 km or more) and can move sideways at considerable speed.
sehor (Ar.)	the meal eaten before dawn during the period of Ramadan (see also *karem*).
tachelt (Tk)	horned viper (*cerastes*).
tagella (Tk)	wheat flour, used to make a form of unleavened bread; a favoured dish of the Kel Ahaggar.
tagelmoust (Tk)	the Tuareg veil (see also *chech*). Traditionally the *tagelmoust* is made from Sudanese indigo-dyed cloth.
tahlé (Tk)	a coarse grass found in Ahaggar (*Typha elephantina*).
Taitok (Tk)	noble descent group of the Kel Ahaggar. Stripped of their

	authority by the French in 1918 for their continued resistance to colonial rule, they settled increasingly in Niger.
Tamahak (Tk)	the Berber language of the Kel Ahaggar.
tamarisk (*tamarix*)	tree found widely throughout Ahaggar.
takouba (Tk)	the traditional Tuareg broad-sword.
tarout (Tk)	ancient cypress (*Cupressus sempervirens* var. *dupreziana*) found in parts of Tassili-n-Ajjer.
tassili (Tk)	plateau (e.g., Tassili-n-Ajjer).
Tegehe-n-Efis (Tk)	vassal descent group of the Kel Ahaggar, traditionally attached to the noble Taitok.
tehergelé (Tk)	aromatic herb used to flavour tea.
tehot (Tk)	the evil eye.
Tidjani	religious order centred at Ain Madhi, to the west of Laghouat.
tifinagh (Tk)	the Tuareg script.
tinhert (Tk)	aromatic herb used to flavour tea.
Tin Hinane (Tk)	legendary ancestress of the Kel Ahaggar.
tisemt (Tk)	salt.
udi (Tk)	soured goat's milk.
ult (Tk)	daughter of (see *ag*).
Uraren	ancient noble descent group of the Ghat/Ajjer region.
zeriba (Ar.)	reed hut or enclosure.

Suggestions for further reading

Henri Lhote, *The Search for the Tassili Frescoes*: published in translation by Hutchinson, 1959; out of print, but available through most large libraries.

Jeremy Keenan, *The Tuareg: People of Ahaggar* (Allen Lane, Penguin Books Ltd, 1977). Out of print, but being republished in 2001 by Sickle Moon Books (available through Sickle Moon Books, 3 Inglebert Street, Clerkenwell, London EC1R 1XR). This gives a detailed history of the Kel Ahaggar and their social and political organisation up to the early 1970s. A new Preface, bridging a thirty-year gap, links the new edition with the original work.

Malika Hachid, *Le Tassili des Ajjer* (Alger and Editions–Paris Méditerranée, 1998; Edif 2000). Probably the best account of the geology, flora, fauna and prehistory of the Tassili-n-Ajjer, especially its rock art; French text with superb colour illustrations (ISBN 2-84272-052-0).

Johannes Nicolaisen & Ida Nicolaisen, *The Pastoral Tuareg: Ecology, Culture and Society* (2 vols) (The Carlsberg Foundation/Rhodos, Copenhagen, 1997). The most comprehensive ethnographic record of the Tuareg. (Available in the UK through Thames and Hudson; ISBN 87 7245 569 1.)

For information about travelling in Ahaggar and the Tassili with the Tuareg, or to contact Bahedi's new travel agency, see www.saharatec.com

Index

Index

Index